C000094461

WHERE THE WORLD MEETS TO PRAY

Daniele Och
UK editor

INVITATIONAL
INTERDENOMINATIONAL
INTERNATIONAL

37 LANGUAGES
Multiple formats are available in some languages

Melanie Tonia Evans . com
N. A. Recovery . Program.

The Bible Reading Fellowship
15 The Chambers, Vineyard
Abingdon OX14 3FE
brf.org.uk

The Bible Reading Fellowship (BRF) is a Registered Charity (233280)

ISBN 978 1 80039 032 4
All rights reserved

Originally published in the USA by The Upper Room® **upperroom.org**
US edition © 2021 The Upper Room, Nashville, TN (USA). All rights reserved.
This edition © The Bible Reading Fellowship 2021
Cover photo by Rebecca J Hall; world map on p. 6 © Thinkstock

Acknowledgements

Scripture quotations marked with the following abbreviations are taken from the
version shown. Where no acronym is given, the quotation is taken from the same
version as the headline reference.

NIV: The Holy Bible, New International Version (Anglicised edition) copyright © 1979,
1984, 2011 by Biblica. Used by permission of Hodder & Stoughton Publishers, an
Hachette UK company. All rights reserved. 'NIV' is a registered trademark of Biblica.
UK trademark number 1448790.

NRSV: The New Revised Standard Version of the Bible, Anglicised Edition, copyright
© 1989, 1995 by the Division of Christian Education of the National Council of the
Churches of Christ in the USA. Used by permission. All rights reserved.

CEB: copyright © 2011 by Common English Bible.

KJV: the Authorised Version of the Bible (The King James Bible), the rights in which
are vested in the Crown, are reproduced by permission of the Crown's Patentee,
Cambridge University Press.

A catalogue record for this book is available from the British Library

Printed by Gutenberg Press, Tarxien, Malta

How to use *The Upper Room*

The Upper Room is ideal in helping us spend a quiet time with God each day. Each daily entry is based on a passage of scripture and is followed by a meditation and prayer. Each person who contributes a meditation to the magazine seeks to relate their experience of God in a way that will help those who use *The Upper Room* every day.

Here are some guidelines to help you make best use of *The Upper Room*:

1 Read the passage of scripture. It is a good idea to read it more than once, in order to have a fuller understanding of what it is about and what you can learn from it.
2 Read the meditation. How does it relate to your own experience? Can you identify with what the writer has outlined from their own experience or understanding?
3 Pray the written prayer. Think about how you can use it to relate to people you know or situations that need your prayers today.
4 Think about the contributor who has written the meditation. Some users of the *The Upper Room* include this person in their prayers for the day.
5 Meditate on the 'Thought for the day' and the 'Prayer focus', perhaps using them again as the focus for prayer or direction for action.

Why is it important to have a daily quiet time? Many people will agree that it is the best way of keeping in touch every day with the God who sustains us and who sends us out to do his will and show his love to the people we encounter each day. Meeting with God in this way reassures us of his presence with us, helps us to discern his will for us and makes us part of his worldwide family of Christian people through our prayers.

I hope that you will be encouraged as you use the magazine regularly as part of your daily devotions, and that God will richly bless you as you read his word and seek to learn more about him.

Daniele Och
UK editor

BRF needs you!

If you're one of our thousands of regular *Upper Room* readers you will know all about the rich rewards of regular Bible reading and the value of daily notes to encourage and inspire you. *Upper Room* readers share those blessings with Christians across the world. They know that every day, in each part of the day, someone, somewhere is reading the same meditation.

If you enjoy reading *The Upper Room*, and love the feeling of being part of a worldwide family, would you be willing to help spread the word about this popular resource? Could you, for example, start an *Upper Room* reading group to introduce your friends or colleagues to the notes, not to take the place of private prayer and reflection but to share insights and grow together.

It doesn't need to be complicated or nerve-wracking: every reflection in *The Upper Room* ends with a question or thought to ponder. And because these reflections are rooted in the personal experience of Christians from every corner of the world, to read and discuss them with others will help to deepen knowledge, strengthen friendships and forge worldwide bonds of faith and fellowship.

We can supply further information if you need it and would love to hear about it if you do start an *Upper Room* reading group.

For more information:

- Email **enquiries@brf.org.uk**
- Telephone BRF on **+44 (0)1865 319700** Mon–Fri 9.30–16.30
- Write to us at BRF, 15 The Chambers, Vineyard, Abingdon OX14 3FE

Co-creating holy space

'You shall make the tabernacle with ten curtains of fine twisted linen, and blue, purple, and crimson yarns; you shall make them with cherubim skilfully worked into them.'

Exodus 26:1 (NRSV)

Our creator calls us into a relationship of careful listening and creativity. Woven among all the detailed instructions about materials and colours associated with building the tabernacle, we find this rather enigmatic statement, 'You shall make them… skilfully.' This directive commands the artists to add in their own thoughtful designs and indicates that God desires an artistic alliance with us!

Julia Cameron, author of *The Artist's Way: A spiritual path to higher creativity*, says, 'When we open ourselves to our creativity, we open ourselves to the Creator's creativity within us and our lives.' And I would also add, this work of opening is integral to God's restorative action in the world around us. To be clear, creativity doesn't always refer to an artistic venture. It may also refer to any endeavour that brings life-giving joy and beauty. For some, balancing an algebraic formula or laying floor tiles can be as joyful as painting, cooking or singing. Whenever and however we choose to develop our creative selves under the grace and guidance of God, we are helping the Lord make room for love and re-creation to take root in our world.

Revd Kimberly Orr
World editor and publisher

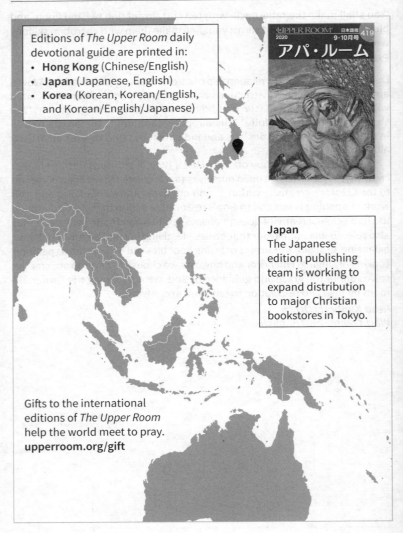

Editions of *The Upper Room* daily devotional guide are printed in:
- **Hong Kong** (Chinese/English)
- **Japan** (Japanese, English)
- **Korea** (Korean, Korean/English, and Korean/English/Japanese)

UPPER ROOM 日本語版 No.
2020 9・10月号 419
アパ・ルーム

Japan
The Japanese edition publishing team is working to expand distribution to major Christian bookstores in Tokyo.

Gifts to the international editions of *The Upper Room* help the world meet to pray.
upperroom.org/gift

The editor writes...

[Jesus] called a little child to him, and placed the child among them. And he said: 'Truly I tell you, unless you change and become like little children, you will never enter the kingdom of heaven.'
Matthew 18:2–3 (NIV)

Recently, I was reading aloud a psalm as part of a time of prayer when I was brought up short by some of the words I was praying. The words were: 'Arise, Lord... Awake, my God; decree justice' (Psalm 7:6–7). I have read and prayed through the Psalms many times over the years, and I realise the sentiment expressed by the psalmist in these verses is found throughout that book. Many of the psalms are pleas for a seemingly passive or distant God to act.

Maybe it was the formality of the language ('Arise', 'decree justice') that made me not notice this before, but it occurred to me that, in praying out these words, I was addressing God effectively in the same way that I sometimes speak to my children – 'Come on; it's time to get up,' I might say to them, or, 'Enough screen time now; you need to tidy your room.' It made me think, 'Am I really prepared to speak to God as if he were a child? Who am I to tell the sovereign Lord to "wake up"? If anything, it should be the other way round.'

Of course, in composing these verses, the psalmist's intention was almost certainly not to address God as a child. Nevertheless, they gave me a fresh appreciation of the grace and humility of our heavenly Father – that in the psalter he has given us prayers in which sometimes we make bold demands for God to act.

This should not come as a surprise when we consider the life of Jesus. In Jesus, we see God become a baby. In Jesus, we see God submit to being obedient to his earthly parents.

I find such humility to be awe-inspiring. But it is also challenging. For in Jesus not only do we see God prepared to become a child, but we also hear the words 'unless you change and become like little children, you will never enter the kingdom of heaven'.

Daniele Och
UK editor

PS – I am delighted to include in this issue the meditation by the winner of BRF's *The Upper Room* writing competition 2020, Andrew Dutton. You can read it on 11 November. The meditations by the two runners-up will feature in the January–April 2022 issue.

Before a breakthrough

Read Joshua 6:1–20

At the seventh time, when the priests had blown the trumpets, Joshua said to the people, 'Shout! For the Lord has given you the city.'
Joshua 6:16 (NRSV)

The heating in our apartment building was completely broken and was unlikely to be repaired for at least 24 hours. As we settled in to wait, every tenant quickly felt the chill of winter.

My husband and I put on extra layers of clothing and thanked God for electricity to cook with and hot water for showering. I was determined to remain positive. But when we woke up the next morning, the flat was even colder than the day before. By midday, I started to wonder if we should go to a hotel or buy portable heaters, but we didn't have the money for either.

Looking for a distraction from the cold, I opened my Bible to Joshua 6. When I read about the Israelites' absolute reliance on God, I was in awe. Instead of shouting in jubilation *after* God gave them their victory, the Israelites shouted in faith *before* the walls fell. With renewed faith in God's provision, I began thanking God. Shortly after this, the heat came back on. Apparently, the necessary part arrived early and the repair was simple. God provided!

Next time I face adversity, I hope to remember this provision and quiet my doubts. Like the Israelites at Jericho, I want to praise God even before I see a breakthrough.

Prayer: *Merciful God, thank you for always being faithful. Teach us to praise you and trust in your deliverance even before we see a breakthrough in our situation. Amen*

Thought for the day: When doubts arise, I will praise the Lord's faithfulness.

Madeline Twooney (North Rhine-Westphalia, Germany)

Child of God

Read Genesis 1:26–31

God saw all that he had made, and it was very good.
Genesis 1:31 (NIV)

Years ago my husband and I adopted our daughter, a young girl from Vietnam whose parents had been lost during the war. Her mother was Vietnamese, her father was black, and she was a beautiful shade of brown.

When she was five years old, we all went to a church picnic, where she immediately left for the playground. But she came running back to us, crying. She told us that some of the children said she couldn't ride on the merry-go-round because she was brown (though that was not the word they used). I felt sick; this was our child! My husband told her she was fine just the way she was and that it was the other kids who had the problem.

Paul wrote in his letter to the Galatians that 'all of you are one in Christ Jesus' (Galatians 3:28). God loves all the children of the world, and as God's children, we are called to love one another.

Prayer: *Thank you, God, for creating all of humankind in your image. Forgive us when we fail to love others the way you love us. Amen*

Thought for the day: All the children of the world are children of God.

Marnie Cotton (Tennessee, USA)

Last days

Read Psalm 121

I lift up my eyes to the hills – from where will my help come? My help comes from the Lord, who made heaven and earth.
Psalm 121:1–2 (NRSV)

My husband, Peter, died in September 2018. On the anniversary of his death, it was a sunny autumn morning, so I went into the garden early to cut a small bunch of roses from the bushes he had planted. Then I walked up to our country churchyard to put them on his cremation stone, which simply records his name and the dates of his birth and death. After tidying the grass edges round his stone, I sat in the church-yard by the great old yew tree and thanked God for our 68 years together and for our wonderful family.

During Peter's final days, the hospice staff showed us immense kindness. This included the chaplain who had called at the hospice, apparently by chance, and came up to see us. As my eldest son, my daughter-in-law and I stood around Peter's bed, the chaplain read Psalm 121 and then prayed with us before laying his hands on Peter in blessing. Peter died peacefully soon afterwards.

In the weeks prior to this, as Peter stoically accepted the pain of his worsening cancer and his inability to move beyond his wheelchair and bed, I too had to adapt to the routine of being his carer. I am truly thankful that I was able to do so, but at the same time my energy often ran low. At that point I found that my help did indeed come from the Lord, as I discovered the prayer below, which sustained me every day.

Prayer: *Encircle us, Lord, in our routine. Keep faithfulness and strength and love within. Keep restlessness without. Encircle us, Lord, in your grace. Amen*

Thought for the day: God will give us the strength we need.

Diana Coldicott (England, United Kingdom)

Together in prayer

Read Romans 12:9–13

Be joyful in hope, patient in affliction, faithful in prayer.
Romans 12:12 (NIV)

Inside the kitchen, popcorn popped and conversation buzzed. We followed our hostess into her lounge as rain pelted the windows. But the orange flames of a log-burner flickered behind glass doors, making the room warm and cosy. We were a small group of women from different denominations who had come together to pray.

Concerns and emotions that had been bottled up for a long time came pouring out. The issues were varied and many, but there was no condemnation. Some spoke of political issues. There were church concerns too, and personal problems that seemed to have no obvious answer. But it was a relief just to express our feelings. There may have been differences among us, but through our praying we were united in love and understanding.

When the meeting was over, we huddled together under a canopy of umbrellas and ventured out into the stormy night. We went our separate ways, but praying as a group knitted us together with a common thread. And in the middle of it all was Jesus.

Prayer: *Thank you, Jesus, for hearing our prayers. We pray as you taught us, 'Our Father in heaven, hallowed be your name, your kingdom come, your will be done on earth as it is in heaven. Give us today our daily bread. Forgive us our debts, as we also have forgiven our debtors. And lead us not into temptation, but deliver us from the evil one.'* Amen*

Thought for the day: Praying with others connects us all to God.

Pauline Pullan (England, United Kingdom)

PRAYER FOCUS: THE GLOBAL CHRISTIAN COMMUNITY
*Matthew 6:9–13

Two little words

Read Matthew 25:14–21

His master replied, 'Well done, good and faithful servant! You have been faithful with a few things; I will put you in charge of many things. Come and share your master's happiness!'
Matthew 25:21 (NIV)

Today's scripture reading describes a master's positive response to a servant who handled instruction and resources well. Verse 21 came to my mind in my weekly small group when we decided that each of us would choose a word that represented our focus for the year. People chose words like 'kindness' and 'love'. But I struggled when making my choice. I knew I needed to focus on my tendency to act on my own, without considering God's will. The word 'submit' scared me, and 'obey' was not quite right either.

This scripture story provided the answer. When I meet my master at the end of my life, I want to hear, 'Well done.' Therefore, instead of one word, I chose the phrase, 'well done'. I am learning to focus on it each day.

Each morning I write down what I consider to have been 'well done' from the day before: helping someone unload a shopping cart, sending 'thinking of you' cards, filling a box with small gifts for a friend after surgery, paying several bills at once, making necessary medical appointments. With all of these I have given attention to being healthy and helpful. On their own they are small; but the overall change in my life's focus has been huge.

Prayer: *O God, we know that you are the way, the truth and the life. Help us turn to you first, before deciding or acting on our own. Amen*

Thought for the day: When I focus my mind and heart on scripture, God can transform my life.

June O. Bond (Maryland, USA)

True joy

Read Romans 5:1–5

Whenever you face trials of any kind, consider it nothing but joy, because you know that the testing of your faith produces endurance; and let endurance have its full effect, so that you may be mature and complete, lacking in nothing.
James 1:2–4 (NRSV)

I have chronic pain that can inhibit me from carrying out everyday activities. I owned my own irrigation business, and I was constantly reminded of the pain in my back. After dealing with pain and stiffness for about a year, I was diagnosed with arthritis in my lower back. For an 18-year-old about to go to university, the diagnosis felt devastating. I questioned God as to why I would have this issue when school and my business were going so well.

But then I saw the bigger picture. I was thinking about what I could do 'on my own' instead of who had given me the talents to succeed. I was focused on the gifts instead of the gift-giver. My arthritis reminds me that true joy isn't found in what I was seeking as a high school senior.

Seemingly devastating circumstances can build our character. As I rely on God to help me deal with my back pain, I am learning endurance through Christ that will help me find true joy in God.

Prayer: *Dear God, thank you for remaining with us through our struggles. Help us to find true joy in you. Amen*

Thought for the day: What challenges have taught me to rely on God?

Jacob Foster (California, USA)

Treasures

Read Matthew 6:19–21

Where your treasure is, there your heart will be also.
Matthew 6:21 (NIV)

When I read about the fire at the iconic Shuri Castle in Okinawa, I was stunned. The main building of the 500-year-old UNESCO World Heritage site burned to ashes in the early hours of 31 October 2019. My family and I had just visited the castle for our vacation in 2018. The magnificent structure was an important landmark of Okinawa's Ryukyu kingdom, and many of the local residents were devastated by the destruction of the castle.

Though I felt sad that such an important historical site had been destroyed in an overnight fire, today's reading came to mind. No matter how much wealth or how many assets we have, they do not last forever. It is more important to build treasures of faith. They cannot be taken away from us, and today's quoted verse reminds us that our treasures reflect what is in our hearts.

Matthew 6:21 is especially comforting in challenging times like the pandemic. Healthcare workers fight valiantly to save lives, and many people are finding ways to help however they can. These people are building treasures that will forever be imprinted on the minds and hearts of many.

Prayer: *Dear Lord, thank you for the reminder that we are just stewards of our earthly possessions, while the treasures we build in our hearts are eternal. Amen*

Thought for the day: What eternal treasures have I stored in my heart?

Agnes Wee (Singapore)

PRAYER FOCUS: THOSE WHO HAVE LOST POSSESSIONS IN A CRISIS

The birdbath

Read James 2:1–8

My brothers and sisters, when you show favouritism you deny the faithfulness of our Lord Jesus Christ.
James 2:1 (CEB)

When I was 54 years old, I moved back home with my mother and sister. During this time, I realised how much I loved birds. I was especially fond of robins.

One day I saw crows taking over the birdbath. I chased them away because I wanted only the robins to enjoy it. After several tries, the crows eventually gave up. About a week later, I saw a number of crows enjoying the water in our neighbour's backyard – water that was coming from an air conditioner. At that moment I felt ashamed for not letting them enjoy the birdbath. After all, the crows had needs just like the other birds, and they deserved to have their needs met.

Later I wondered, 'Is that how we treat some people?' God respects no one person over another. If we are Christ-followers, neither should we. I hope that this experience will help me remember to treat all people the same, no matter what race, religion or nationality. We are all God's creation and need God's help. Likewise, God wants us to join in meeting the needs of all God's people, wherever we may find them.

Prayer: *Our heavenly Father, when we interact with others, help us to remember that we are all your creation. Help us all to love one another as you have loved us. Amen*

Thought for the day: Today I will try to see everyone as God does.

Phyllis A. Edwards (North Carolina, USA)

Why not you?

Read Exodus 4:1–17

Do not be anxious about anything, but in every situation, by prayer and petition, with thanksgiving, present your requests to God.
Philippians 4:6 (NIV)

When I was young, I was shy, and my stutter made it worse. School was hard for me, because I could not read a page out loud without pausing or stuttering. I thought of myself as inferior to the other kids. When I had to present a project, I always thought that my classmates would make fun of me. I believed that I wouldn't be able to serve God, because I couldn't speak properly.

But one day, my Sunday school teacher told us the story of the burning bush. God called Moses to lead the people out of Egypt. Moses quickly declined, claiming that he was not the one to lead God's people. He said that he was slow of speech. God told him not to worry, because God would make sure he was surrounded by the right people.

My whole mindset changed. I realised that God can work through anyone. As I grew up and went on mission trips, I took this passage to heart and did what God wanted me to do without fear. With God by my side, I went to nearby states with my youth group to spread the gospel.

No matter what problems we face, we don't have to let them hold us back from spreading God's word. God has great plans for us, and we just have to listen to God.

Prayer: *Heavenly Father, no matter what we have done or what problems we have, help us to remember that you have chosen us to participate in your wonderful plan. Amen*

Thought for the day: God has great plans in store for me.

Benjamin Medellin Jr (Texas, USA)

Great love

Read Romans 5:6–8

For God so loved the world that he gave his one and only Son, that whoever believes in him shall not perish but have eternal life.
John 3:16 (NIV)

Around the time my firstborn celebrated her 19th birthday, I became pregnant with my second child. Complications during the pregnancy led to a caesarean birth. My son remained in a neonatal care unit for six days. Since his birth two years ago, I have never stopped thanking God for the gift of my son, his health and the joy of being a mother to a young child again.

One day, after some reflection during my prayer time, I realised that I would be willing to give my life for my children. In that moment, I began to understand the enormous sacrifice God made to give his only Son for the sins of humankind. I would be willing to give my life for my children, but I would find it unthinkable to sacrifice my children for anyone. Only God was able to do it. And only Christ was able to be faithful to that call. The apostle Paul writes: 'God demonstrates his own love for us in this: While we were still sinners, Christ died for us.' What incredible and amazing love!

Prayer: *Loving God, thank you for your infinite love that truly surpasses all understanding. Help us to feel this love that is the same yesterday, today and through eternity. Amen*

Thought for the day: How do I reciprocate God's love for me?

Azalia Alecón (Dominican Republic)

Responding in love

Read Matthew 5:38–42

*Do not resist an evildoer. But if anyone strikes you on the right cheek,
turn the other also.*
Matthew 5:39 (NRSV)

My older brother ran down the stairs with tears streaming from his eyes.
A few seconds later I followed, trying to keep up with him on my little,
three-year-old legs. When my brother and I entered the living room, my
mum was startled and concerned. She asked my brother, 'What's wrong?
Why are you crying?' My brother answered through his tears, 'Grant hit
me for no reason!' Before my mum had a chance to respond, I exclaimed,
'That is not true! He is lying! I didn't hit him for no reason; I *kicked* him for
no reason!' This story from my childhood makes me laugh, but I also feel
bad about the way I treated my brother. He didn't deserve it.

Sometimes we're treated in ways we don't deserve. Whether a friend
abandons us, a co-worker gossips about us, a family member manipu-
lates us or a boss undervalues us, our tendency is to retaliate. But Jesus
calls his followers to respond differently.

In today's reading, Jesus speaks about how his listeners have twisted
God's words to justify revenge. But then Jesus urges his followers to
respond in a different way. Even when we're treated in ways that we
don't deserve, Jesus calls us to respond with love.

Prayer: *Dear Lord, thank you for the way you love us. Give us the
strength to respond to others with love. Amen*

Thought for the day: Even when I want to retaliate, I will respond with
love.

Grant Roth (Missouri, USA)

A grandmother's legacy

Read Deuteronomy 6:4–9

Keep these words that I am commanding you today in your heart. Recite them to your children and talk about them when you are at home and when you are away, when you lie down and when you rise.
Deuteronomy 6:6–7 (NRSV)

Over 60 years ago, following a family tragedy, my brother and I moved in with our grandparents. I was eight years old, and it was a significant emotional adjustment. Reading *The Upper Room*, which I found on my grandmother's nightstand, guided me through those years. Through those readings and my grandmother's love, Jesus became real to me.

My grandmother worked hard to care for my brother and me, especially after our grandfather died when I was 13. Imagine being 70 years old and facing the daunting task of raising two teenagers alone! But she knew she was never alone. She had Jesus, and she never let us forget how much we were loved – by Jesus and by her.

When I became a mum, I was determined to instill God's word in the lives of my children. No matter our struggles, I always knew where to turn for help and reminded my children that we always have a direct line to God through prayer.

Now I'm praising God for grandchildren. They are the joy of my life. I praise God for the lessons I learned from a loving grandmother and from time spent with *The Upper Room*.

Prayer: *Thank you, loving God, for parents and grandparents who create a positive, everlasting influence on their children by centering their lives on your word. Amen*

Thought for the day: Because of Jesus' love for me, I always have love to give.

Dona Bakker (California, USA)

Finishing strong

Read Luke 12:22–34

[Jesus] said to his disciples, 'Therefore I tell you, do not worry about your life, what you will eat, or about your body, what you will wear.'
Luke 12:22 (NRSV)

When I was admitted to a university for a five-year course in agricultural extension and rural development, my family was at a low point financially. My mother spent much of her business capital to pay for my expenses. My father encouraged me to focus on my studies.

My circumstances became increasingly difficult, and I became more and more gloomy. In my isolation, I began to write, entering writing competitions hoping to win prize money that did not come. But I was learning to trust God more.

After I had spent years faithfully waiting, God came through for me. I received a one-year scholarship in my third year that covered my tuition. By the end of my fourth year, my academic journey became less cumbersome because God sent sponsors who paid for my books, my daily cab fare and my research work. They were total strangers; our only connection was our Christian faith. Through this connection, a warm friendship blossomed between us.

Though my studies suffered because of my financial struggles, I was able to finish with high grades. I am full of gratitude to God, who made my end better than my small beginning.

Prayer: *Dear God, thank you for the ways you provide for us through others. Help us to do your work and provide for others when we can. Amen*

Thought for the day: God provides for me through the kindness of others.

Ehi-kowochio Ogwiji (Federal Capital Territory, Nigeria)

God's enduring love

Read Psalm 103:7–18

The Lord's faithful love is from forever ago to forever from now for those who honour him.
Psalm 103:17 (CEB)

I love the beach. Whether the sun is shining or it's cloudy and rainy, the smell of the salt water, the endless view and the sound of breaking waves soothe my soul. The breaking of the waves and vastness of the ocean are assurances for me of God's steadfastness and presence.

Over the years, I've collected boxes of seashells. Now I allow myself one shell per visit. On my last visit, while I was walking along the beach, a shiny shell caught my eye. But when I picked it up and looked closer, I saw that it had a hole in it and was scarred by tiny stones embedded in it. I tossed it aside but felt a little nudge I couldn't explain. I picked up the shell again and brushed off all the sand.

It occurred to me how much my life was like that shell – certainly far from perfect. But despite my imperfections, God has never cast me aside. That shell now sits on my desk next to my Bible as a daily reminder that God loves me just as I am.

Prayer: *Heavenly Father, thank you for the assurance that you will never toss us aside. Thank you for loving us just as we are. Amen*

Thought for the day: Despite my imperfections, God will always love me.

Phyllis J. Brockwell (Virginia, USA)

Hope and a future

Read 1 Timothy 4:7–16

Let no one despise your youth, but set the believers an example in speech and conduct, in love, in faith, in purity.
1 Timothy 4:12 (NRSV)

When my son was in kindergarten, I started a morning ritual of reading *The Upper Room* to him. Though we were often rushed in the mornings getting ready for school and work, it became meaningful for us to make time for Jesus and to spend time as a family.

When he was younger, I wondered if some of the topics, such as death, illness or even questioning of faith, might have been too mature or complex for him. But I realised that in this world of troubled times, teaching my son about the Bible and equipping him with an armour of salvation is important.

Upon hearing that he has treated others fairly or defended a playmate whom someone else has treated unkindly, I have realised that the grace of the Lord is key to his life. As a parent I have witnessed a lot of my child's joys and sorrows, but having a strong faith has been a source of encouragement for us as a family. As we weather the storms of life, I am assured that the Lord will be by our side, just as we read in Isaiah 66:13, 'As a mother comforts her child, so I will comfort you.'

Prayer: *Loving God, as we grow in an ever-changing and sometimes unjust world, renew our strength daily. Walk with us and help us to be a light for others. Amen*

Thought for the day: When I spend time in prayer and Bible reading, I renew my strength.

Melissa Yamaguchi (Hawaii, USA)

Beyond understanding

Read Job 38:1–7

Have you comprehended the vast expanses of the earth? Tell me, if you know all this.
Job 38:18 (NIV)

One morning I met up with my instructor at the scientific complex of our college, and we went to the room where our transmission electron microscope is kept. In the dim room my instructor showed me the controls, and we started to view our sample. Looking at the computer monitor of the microscope, the image started to zoom in, and suddenly I could see the atomic structure of the sample!

The image was so different than anything we can see with our eyes alone. It made me think about how imperfect our understanding of the universe is. We are limited beings with limited comprehension.

God, who created the universe and whose knowledge is far beyond our own, calls us to be humble and open to opinions or answers that may challenge our own perspective. When we remember our limited understanding, we can be more patient with people whose understanding and beliefs are different from our own.

Prayer: *Dear God, help us understand our smallness and be humble to know how to respect people whose understanding and beliefs are different from ours. In Jesus' name. Amen*

Thought for the day: Only God's understanding is perfect.

Marçal Ainsa i Bertran (Catalonia, Spain)

A balanced life

Read Psalm 16:1–11

Seek ye the kingdom of God; and all these things shall be added unto you.

Luke 12:31 (KJV)

In aerobics class I learned a new exercise that incorporates stretching and balance. A deep lunge forward is followed by rising up on one's toes and pausing, arms extended outward. It was easy until I got distracted. Suddenly, balancing was not so easy. In that moment, the instructor said, 'If you lose your balance, just reset and begin again.' I did, and – just like that – my sense of balance returned.

How many times do we get distracted in our daily lives and lose our balance? I am coming to realise how often I need to pause in this crazy, busy, wonderful life to reset and find my balance. No matter how organised and disciplined we feel when we rise each day, distractions come our way. When we make time to reset through prayer and scripture reading – to seek God's guidance, comfort and inspiration – we can walk in faith with God.

Prayer: *Father God, as we go about our busy days, draw us close to you. Help us seek your will and walk in your way. As Jesus taught us, we pray, 'Our Father which art in heaven, Hallowed be thy name. Thy kingdom come. Thy will be done in earth, as it is in heaven. Give us this day our daily bread. And forgive us our debts, as we forgive our debtors. And lead us not into temptation, but deliver us from evil: For thine is the kingdom, and the power, and the glory, for ever.'* Amen*

Thought for the day: When I get distracted, I can reset by seeking God first.

Belinda Jo 'B.J.' Mathias (Mississippi, USA)

Making a way

Read Isaiah 12:2–5

Sing to the Lord, for he has done glorious things; let this be known to all the world.
Isaiah 12:5 (NIV)

In January, I made the difficult decision to leave my job. After completing my paralegal certification in February, I began looking for a job, sending out application after application. I felt like something good would happen soon; but it didn't.

I had great interviews and gained valuable experience, but I still found myself without a job. As time wore on, I felt as though God had abandoned me. I was stepping out in faith and applying for positions everywhere I could, but none of the doors on which I was knocking opened. Seven months later, however, God answered my prayer and opened a door for me at a lumberyard in the town where I live.

Today's reading reminds us that we can trust God and that we should praise God's glorious work in the world. Working at a lumberyard wasn't the job I was hoping for, but I praise God for making a way for me. When God does something incredible and delivers us into a new season, we can praise God and share God's goodness with everyone.

Prayer: *Heavenly Father, thank you for making a way for us when there seems to be no way forward. Help us to trust in you as we wait. In Jesus' name. Amen*

Thought for the day: I will praise God for making a way in my life.

Michael Kimmel (Texas, USA)

The vulnerability of love

Read John 13:1–17

I have set you an example that you should do as I have done for you.
John 13:15 (NIV)

I was kneeling on the floor, holding a long, green sock. A few days earlier, my husband had undergone knee-replacement surgery, and it was my job to change the special compression socks recommended by the hospital. We both found this to be quite an ordeal! The socks were non-stretchy and difficult to maneuver over the heel, and I was afraid my clumsy attempts would cause him even more pain. Yet, somehow, we found ourselves laughing at the absurdity as we pulled and smoothed and sweated, feeling so helpless yet brought so close.

I had a strange sense of Jesus kneeling beside me, cradling that vulnerable foot, maneuvering the sock gently upward. He seemed to say to me, 'This is love lavished on what is hurting, soiled or lost. This is my love for you to give.' As I felt my husband's trust in me, I realised how vulnerable the love of Jesus makes us – exposing our embarrassment and awkwardness, yet giving a real insight into the sacrificial love of God. Jesus asks us to do as he did – not necessarily in washing feet but in humbly and patiently caring for one another in whatever ways are needed. It's not easy, but I believe this kind of love lies at the heart of being a follower of Jesus.

Prayer: *Father God, thank you for your love for us. Help us to share your loving care with someone today. Amen*

Thought for the day: Letting someone care for me is an act of love.

April McIntyre (England, United Kingdom)

Facing change

Read Jeremiah 29:10–14

I know the plans I have for you, says the Lord, plans for your welfare and not for harm, to give you a future with hope.
Jeremiah 29:11 (NRSV)

I watched my mum cry before I turned and walked away, off to my university dorm. I was the first to leave, and she couldn't handle it. I nearly couldn't either. Besides the hard goodbyes from my parents and sister, I also had to say goodbye to lifelong friends, my childhood home and all of their familiar comforts. I knew that the next time I went back, things would be different. Friends who stayed behind would have moved on, and the relationship I had with my family would not be the same. Despite phone calls and text messages, I already felt a sense of separation.

I struggled with the idea of my life changing so rapidly. I prayed, reflected and asked God for guidance. Just as the disciples had to accept that Jesus was leaving and that their former way of life was over, I had to remember that God led me here, and I followed.

Although the goodbyes were tough, I know they prepared me for my future. Knowing that changes are part of God's plan for me has made me grateful and optimistic. God is with us every step we take, even if that step is in a new direction.

Prayer: *Dear God, remind us to trust in you and remain positive in the face of change. Keep us on the path of righteousness as we work to accomplish the goals you have set for us. Amen*

Thought for the day: Change is part of God's good plan for my life.

Collin Kelly (Texas, USA)

Called to help

Read 1 Kings 17:1–6

You will drink from the brook, and I have directed the ravens to supply you with food there.
1 Kings 17:4 (NIV)

In today's reading, after Elijah commanded a drought, God made all the arrangements for Elijah to survive. It is amazing to me how God takes care of God's people. I imagine that Elijah was surprised to hear that God had chosen ravens as his benefactors, but I am sure he was grateful for their daily delivery of meat and bread.

Unexpected benefactors have also blessed me. Once a woman sent me a cheque for the exact amount of money I desperately needed to fix my car. She had no clue I needed it, and I had never done much to bless her. Nevertheless, she acted on her faith and was obedient to God's call to offer help.

Many people around the world are dealing with the loss of loved ones, their own health, financial security or even just peace of mind. I know God can and will perform miracles. Though many of us have felt and may still feel like Elijah, perhaps it is our turn to be the ravens. God may call us to buy food, make car payments, clean homes, teach children, pray and cry for friends and strangers. We show our faithfulness when we listen and obey God's call for us to be benefactors.

Prayer: *God of all the world, make us channels of your blessings. Help us seize every opportunity to show your love to the people around us. Help us be the ravens who provide for your servants. Amen*

Thought for the day: How will I answer God's call to provide for others today?

Frances Huezo (California, USA)

Let us be one

Read Psalm 133:1–3

Behold, how good and how pleasant it is for brethren to dwell together in unity!
Psalm 133:1 (KJV)

During my first stay outside of my country, I attended a church of a different denomination from my own. I enjoyed months of Communion and traditional hymns with the congregation. When I returned to my church, I began to worship once again with the music of contemporary bands. The sermons of the church I had visited were presented in a calm manner and ended with a simple prayer. In contrast, the sermons of my home church became intense and ended with a worship time filled with cries of repentance and adoration. I did not feel out of place in either church.

The change of worship style made me reflect on the greatness of God who created us so different and yet so similar. There is no perfect church or liturgy, no singular way to worship – God takes pleasure in believers who have learned to live together in harmony (see Psalm 133), testifying to the world about God's love (see John 17:23). Christians, no matter where we congregate – let us be one!

Prayer: *Dear God, help us to contribute to the unity of your church and to live in harmony with others. Amen*

Thought for the day: I glorify God when I live in love and unity with others.

Roberto Fernández-Acosta (Havana, Cuba)

Dark night with God

Read Genesis 32:22–30

I will give you the treasures of darkness and riches hidden in secret places, so that you may know that it is I, the Lord, the God of Israel, who call you by your name.
Isaiah 45:3 (NRSV)

On a Saturday morning several years ago, my best friend died in an accident. I spent much of the day with his family, but it wasn't until that night in bed, alone in the dark, that I was truly struck by the impact of losing him. I cried out to God through my tears but felt no response. I wondered if God had turned a deaf ear. Finally, I remembered how Jacob told the angel, 'I will not let you go, unless you bless me' (Genesis 32:26). So I prayed, 'God, I know you are there, and I will hold on until you answer me.' At that moment I was suddenly flooded with an overwhelming sense of God's presence and peace. I will always remember the power and intimacy of that dark night with God.

If we talk to people of faith who have experienced some of life's darkest places, we discover a strange truth: it is in those places that they more clearly saw some of God's most precious treasures. They may tell you that in times of relentless pain or sickness they discovered the love and comfort of God in ways they can't explain.

Some of God's most valuable gifts are revealed in the darkness. Because God is always with us, even the most painful experiences can contain life-changing treasure.

Prayer: *Dear God, make your presence powerfully known to us when we are despairing. Bring us to new life through Christ. Amen*

Thought for the day: I find some of God's most valuable gifts in places I least expect.

Valerie Bryant Bennett (Tennessee, USA)

Patient gardener

Read Luke 13:6–9

Be patient, therefore, beloved, until the coming of the Lord. The farmer waits for the precious crop from the earth, being patient with it until it receives the early and the late rains.
James 5:7 (NRSV)

My father was quite the backyard gardener. Vegetables and fruit trees shared a small rectangular plot. He planted every spring, and he harvested through summer and autumn.

When my father died, I was determined to secure a clipping from his fig bush. A cousin helped me take a clipping and root it. Gradually, the clipping turned into a small seedling. I planted this seedling in my backyard, where it has flourished. Usually by late summer, the fig's limbs are loaded with fruit. Every fall, I prune the fig back from its overgrown summer size. I worry every winter whether it will survive.

As winter becomes spring, I check the base of the fig for a green shoot of life. For weeks, I see no sign of survival. Relief flows over me as I find the first tiny green bud protruding from the trunk.

Being patient can be a challenge. In Luke 13, the impatient vineyard owner wants to give up on the barren fig tree. But the patient gardener requests more time to prune, till and feed the fig. Unlike the impatient vineyard owner, God never loses patience with me.

God's work in us never wavers. God's compassion, wisdom, love and forgiveness are available to sustain us no matter the season.

Prayer: *Father of us all, thank you for not losing patience with us. Sustain us like the patient gardener. Amen*

Thought for the day: Even when I'm impatient, God is patient with me.

Bill Pike (Virginia, USA)

Practice makes perfect

Read Philippians 4:4–9

Whatever is true, whatever is honourable, whatever is just, whatever is pure, whatever is pleasing, whatever is commendable, if there is any excellence and if there is anything worthy of praise, think about these things.
Philippians 4:8 (NRSV)

A friend expressed surprise when I played a Chopin waltz after decades of neglecting the piano. I explained that it was muscle memory – the reason why we all can quickly recall certain abilities learned through repeated motions.

'Practice makes perfect,' my mother used to say as she made sure I did my daily half hour of piano exercises – or whenever I struggled to learn a new skill. Of course, she was right. Repetitive actions become embedded in our memory until they are automatic. This explains why we can still remember multiplication tables or how to ride a bicycle, even years later.

But there is also a kind of practice that makes *imperfect*: repeated negative thoughts. Complaining, criticising and dwelling on anxious or bitter thoughts can become ingrained in our minds. God has been speaking to me about certain negative thought patterns that are not pleasing to God. By 'thought-stopping' – rejecting such thoughts the moment they present themselves – and asking God to transform me through the renewing of my mind (see Romans 12:2), I am learning to overcome this bad habit with one that brings me closer to God instead.

Prayer: *Dear God, thank you for your patience with us. Help us as we work to rid our minds of negative thoughts and instead focus on you. Amen*

Thought for the day: Today I will practise focusing on what pleases God.

Marianne Jones (Ontario, Canada)

Miss Mable

Read Matthew 19:13–15

Start children off on the way they should go, and even when they are old they will not turn from it.
Proverbs 22:6 (NIV)

After nearly 70 years I still have a clear memory of the nursery class in my childhood church. Miss Mable made the Bible stories come alive for us. She let us help tell the story as we placed felt-backed cutout figures of Bible characters on a board covered with flannel. When she told us the story of Noah and the ark, we loved deciding where to place the lions and donkeys and other animals on the ark. I am eternally grateful to Miss Mable for her patient, loving instruction, but her love for each of us was even more important and helped us begin to understand the unconditional love of God.

When I was struggling with my faith as a young adult, I remembered the love of Miss Mable and the other people in that church. On a return visit, I was warmly welcomed. My life was transformed by seeing the gospel lived out in others' lives.

Prayer: *Thank you, Lord, for children. Guide those who teach them with your love and grace. Help us to encourage and support others who lead children in learning about Jesus. Amen*

Thought for the day: How am I living the gospel for others to see?

Jim Harris (Virginia, USA)

Serve Jesus today

Read Matthew 25:31–40

Truly I tell you, just as you did it to one of the least of these who are members of my family, you did it to me.
Matthew 25:40 (NRSV)

As a pastor, I am always looking for ways to serve others. Sometimes that yearning transports my mind to faraway places, and I imagine the strangers I might encounter there. I often wonder, 'How can I prepare to serve people well in the name of Jesus?'

In a season when I was feeling disappointed about my ministry, I wondered whether I was fulfilling my life's purpose and calling. That day, I heard someone say that our purpose is to help others go through life. The next morning, as I prepared breakfast and lunches, I helped my five-year-old get ready for school, gave her medicine, comforted her and made sure she was wearing enough clothes for the cold weather. Amid this sacred chaos, it dawned on me: I am here to serve her in Jesus' name.

That morning, I remembered that our purpose as Christians is to help those closest to us in any moment. Helping others in faraway places is important, but we are Jesus' diligent hands and feet every day in all the places we find ourselves.

Prayer: *Loving Jesus, help us be present to those closest to us today so that our service may be a reminder of your love for the world. Amen*

Thought for the day: Every day holds opportunities to serve God.

Teresita Matos-Post (Florida, USA)

Strengthened

Read 2 Timothy 4:14–18

The Lord stood at my side and gave me strength, so that through me the message might be fully proclaimed and all the Gentiles might hear it. And I was delivered from the lion's mouth.
2 Timothy 4:17 (NIV)

I moved every chair near me in the conference room, but my handbag was not where I had left it. My heart raced as I walked through the rows of chairs. I finally found my handbag shoved under a chair in the last row, wide open. My two wallets had been stolen. I told some of the leaders and ushers at the event. I could not believe this was happening to me.

As people commented on my situation, I started blaming myself for not being careful enough. No one seemed to understand how hard it was for me to come to terms with the fact that my wallets were gone. But some people, like my friend Michelle and my mum, were compassionate and assisted me financially, and 'the Lord stood at my side and gave me strength' (2 Timothy 4:17). God's presence was especially comforting when I was alone and thinking about the unfortunate event that had happened to me.

As I continued to meditate on this verse, I managed to recover and trust in God's power to restore. Sometimes no one understands what we are going through, but we can rest assured that the Lord will stand by us always and give us the strength we need.

Prayer: *Dear Lord, thank you for standing by us and giving us strength. In Jesus' name. Amen*

Thought for the day: When I am feeling drained, I remember that the Lord is nearby to give me strength.

Vimbai Chizarura (Mashonaland East, Zimbabwe)

Listening

Read Luke 10:38–42

'Martha, Martha,' the Lord answered, 'you are worried and upset about many things, but few things are needed – or indeed only one. Mary has chosen what is better, and it will not be taken away from her.'

Luke 10:41-42 (NIV)

In today's reading, Martha wanted to offer Jesus the best hospitality, and she expected a little help from Mary in the kitchen. However, Mary wanted to sit at the feet of Jesus and listen to what he had to say. This story reminds us that hospitality means more than offering refreshments and meals. It is about offering our presence and listening to one another with a compassionate heart.

I learned to practise this kind of hospitality when I volunteered for a month in Sri Lanka in 2004 after a tsunami. As part of the relief efforts, I offered comfort and counselling services to some of those whose loved ones had died in the tragedy. I listened as one woman told me that the tsunami waves had swallowed her husband. When I asked whether she and her two children had received any support from the local church, she said that anyone who came from the church just spouted off religious jargon. Their visits didn't mean much to her because they did not want to listen. Listening is a spiritual gift. All of us can practise the spiritual skill of offering hospitality by listening well.

Prayer: *Dear God, help us to be good listeners to everyone we encounter today. Amen*

Thought for the day: Listening is a spiritual gift that I can offer someone today.

S. Thevanesan (New York, USA)

Never alone

Read Romans 1:8–12

This is the boldness we have in [the Son of God], that if we ask anything according to his will, he hears us.
1 John 5:14 (NRSV)

As I sat in the pew for the worship service, I thought about how disconnected I felt. My daughter is grown and now makes her home in another state, so I now go to church by myself. The connections we made together during her school years have faded, leaving me feeling isolated.

Perhaps my thoughts were an unspoken prayer, because just as the service ended, a woman sitting near me greeted me and reminded me that I'd met her at her place of business years before. If ever there was an answer to a prayer, that simple greeting felt like one. I left feeling grateful and a bit less lonely.

I know that God answers prayers; while I wasn't consciously praying about my loneliness, God answered my need. Often I have felt that my problems are too insignificant to bother God with, but this encounter reminded me that God does care about even the smallest problems we face and will intervene in our lives when we need it.

Prayer: *Dear God, thank you for answering our prayers in unexpected ways. May we be the answer to someone's prayer today. Amen*

Thought for the day: God will answer my prayers – sometimes when I least expect it.

Nanci Lamar (Tennessee, USA)

God's guidance

Read Joshua 1:1–9

Teach me, Lord, the way of your decrees, that I may follow it to the end. Give me understanding, so that I may keep your law and obey it with all my heart. Direct me in the path of your commands, for there I find delight.

Psalm 119:33–35 (NIV)

I worked for several years as a professor and tutored engineering students. My role was to guide students in their course work so that at the end of the semester they could fulfil the project requirements for the year. The majority of the students attended the tutoring sessions regularly and had excellent results. However, one student did not take advantage of the tutoring process, and his project was not approved by the review board.

We often neglect or put off our spiritual health by minimising the time we spend with God and studying God's word. But God is there to guide us. Today's reading from Joshua reminds us to keep God's word prominent in our life. Every day is an opportunity to invest time in our faith, explore scripture and be open to the guidance God sets before us. These practices will enrich our lives and glorify God.

Prayer: *O God, forgive us when we fail to prioritise time with you. Write your word on our hearts and increase our understanding so that we will always be open to your guidance. Amen*

Thought for the day: Today I will seek and follow God's guidance.

Lily Castro (Madrid, Spain)

Beauty in the details

Read 1 Samuel 16:4–7

God doesn't look at things like humans do. Humans see only what is visible to the eyes, but the Lord sees into the heart.
1 Samuel 16:7 (CEB)

Since I have been in prison, my daughter has sent me several drawings. One of my favourites is a self-portrait she drew when she was four years old. To anyone else it probably looks like a bunch of shapes: circles, triangles, ovals and squares that she assembled to form a human body. But I notice much more detail – pupils and irises in the eyes, eyelashes, tennis shoes, a pretty red triangle dress and black rectangle tights. To my eyes, it is better than the *Mona Lisa*, and I treasure her drawing.

Likewise, we have a heavenly Father who looks at our small, daily actions and is pleased when we reflect him there. After all, it's the small details that can make a huge difference in someone's day – shaking someone's hand, speaking an encouraging word, saying hello to someone. Each of these can brighten another person's life in ways we may never know.

We can all take the time today to show kindness to someone in small ways. By doing so, we bring glory to God, who notices and cares about the details in our lives.

Prayer: *Dear God, help us show kindness to everyone we meet today. Amen*

Thought for the day: I can reflect God's love by taking time to notice others.

Steven Paul Simmons (Texas, USA)

Every step

Read Luke 9:23–27

[Jesus] said to them all, If any man will come after me, let him deny himself, and take up his cross daily, and follow me.
Luke 9:23 (KJV)

For over a decade, on the afternoon of World Communion Sunday, I have participated in a hunger walk to raise money for our local food bank and worldwide hunger relief programmes. Each year, congregations from various denominations, members of civic organisations and local school groups gather in one place to begin a journey of awareness. As we walk, we think of those who must embark on long journeys each day to gather food and water, and we think of those who must walk miles each day to their jobs. When I reach the finish line, I am always exhausted. I get a glimpse of what it might be like to walk in someone else's shoes.

Shortly after feeding the multitudes, Jesus tells his followers to take up their crosses daily and follow him. This task requires great commitment. Just as the participants of the hunger walk make an effort to walk in the shoes of the hungry, Christians must take up their crosses daily to walk in the shoes of Jesus. We agree to make this journey in faith, not knowing where the road may lead or how difficult it may get. However, we are assured that we do not make the journey alone. Our Saviour is with us every step of the way.

Prayer: *Dear Lord Jesus, help us to take up our crosses daily and follow you. Give us compassion for those in need, and give us strength when the journey is difficult. Amen*

Thought for the day: I never walk alone when I walk with Christ.

Sherri Tuck (Virginia, USA)

A wise man's legacy

Read Deuteronomy 11:18–23

A good person leaves an inheritance for their children's children.
Proverbs 13:22 (NIV)

It was slow and tedious searching the many secondhand shops, but at last I found what I wanted: a heavy, blue children's Bible, long out of print. It was battered and missing its outer cover, but I recognised every picture inside. This was a copy of the Bible that my father had read to me and my siblings when we were children. I now had children of my own, and this Bible would last us many years.

My father died at the age of 71, before my sons can remember. But soon after my father died, my occasional Bible reading with my boys became a nightly routine in memory of my father's love, devotion and faith. I would read, question, listen and explain. Then we would look at the pictures and share prayers.

My children, now teenagers, still gather every evening for our Bible reading and discussion. As we revisit well-known narratives, we share new levels of understanding and possible interpretations; we discuss our own desires versus God's will for our lives; we apply biblical principles to our current challenges. It is a habit now, a time of shared contemplation and a necessary part of our day. This is my father's legacy.

Prayer: *Dear Lord, place your truth in our hearts through the reading of your word so that we may carry your wisdom and comfort throughout life. Amen*

Thought for the day: How will I share my faith with younger generations?

Fiona M. Jones (Scotland, United Kingdom)

A daily task

Read Romans 12:1–3

Do not conform to the pattern of this world, but be transformed by the renewing of your mind. Then you will be able to test and approve what God's will is – his good, pleasing and perfect will.
Romans 12:2 (NIV)

While scrubbing my kitchen floor one day, I noticed that my faithful old brush was beginning to lose some of its bristles. It was tired and worn and not doing its job properly any more. I realised that it must have been like this for some time, but I simply had not noticed. I had just gone along using it in the same old way without realising that it just wasn't good enough any more.

It occurred to me that we can be like that in our Christian faith. We can form a habit of praying the same old prayers or singing the same old hymns without really paying full attention to them. When that happens, the prayers and songs will not be fulfilling their purpose, which is to praise God and to deepen our relationship with him.

At these times we can follow Paul's advice to renew our minds, get out of the rut and change our way of thinking and behaving. If we do not refresh our worship regularly, it can, like my old scrubbing brush, become mediocre through habit and frequent use.

Prayer: *Father God, let us always be open to change, so that we may continue to serve you with thanksgiving in our world today. Amen*

Thought for the day: Are there any old habits that God wants me to change today?

Kathleen Sharps (England, United Kingdom)

The ordinary

Read Psalm 34:17–20

May the Lord answer you when you are in distress; may the name of the God of Jacob protect you.
Psalm 20:1 (NIV)

One night, I noticed some recurring medical symptoms that concerned me enough that I planned to call my doctor the next morning. For much of the evening, however, I was distraught – pacing the floor and imagining the worst.

As I talked with the Lord about it, I noticed my attention shift to gratitude. I was grateful for the ability to connect with God as a close friend. These reflections eased my distress. I felt God in the ordinary moments of my evening as well: preparing a meal, washing the dishes and walking to the shops. These simple activities provided me with a sense of balance and comfort.

God answered my prayers for peace that night, and I knew God would continue to be with me. I was not disappointed. In the following days, I watched again and again as the Lord worked through everyday moments to show me love: the happy greetings of my neighbour's dog, soothing cups of tea, hot showers and peaceful rest at night. Just as Jesus used bread and wine as an invitation into his everlasting love (see Matthew 26:26–30), God continues to draw close to us through the ordinary. With God's blessing, the ordinary becomes an instrument of healing, restoration and hope.

Prayer: *Dear Lord, thank you for transforming our commonplace routines and experiences into conduits for your peace. Give us eyes to see your presence all around us. Amen*

Thought for the day: God's peace is available in ordinary moments.

Victoria Walsh (Montana, USA)

Eternal life

Read John 4:9–14

The water I give them will become in them a spring of water welling up to eternal life.

John 4:14 (NIV)

My wife had a doctor's appointment, so I accompanied her on the bus ride. Along the way we passed a park, and I noticed a fountain. Perched on its edge were several pigeons who had been drawn to the fresh water fountain to quench their thirst. They drank trustingly, and no one bothered them. It was wonderful to see these creatures enjoy the benefits and access to water.

After we returned home, during my prayer time with God, the image of the fountain remained with me. I searched the Bible and found today's reading. I felt God was leading me to this message. Just as the pigeons were drinking water trustingly from the fountain, Jesus offers us the gift of the water of eternal life. We will not thirst after worldly things that perish because the living water God offers is eternal. Our spiritual thirst will be satisfied.

Prayer: *Giver of life eternal, thank you for offering the gift of living water to satisfy our souls. We pray the prayer Jesus taught us, 'Our Father which art in heaven, Hallowed be thy name. Thy kingdom come. Thy will be done, as in heaven, so in earth. Give us day by day our daily bread. And forgive us our sins; for we also forgive every one that is indebted to us. And lead us not into temptation; but deliver us from evil.'* Amen*

Thought for the day: 'My soul thirsts for God, for the living God' (Psalm 42:2).

Alberto Jerónimo Quesada (Santiago, Chile)

PRAYER FOCUS: THOSE WITHOUT ACCESS TO CLEAN WATER
*Luke 11:2–4 (KJV)

Searching for God

Read Psalm 42:1–11

As a deer longs for flowing streams, so my soul longs for you, O God.
Psalm 42:1 (NRSV)

I had always started my days early with a morning devotional. But everything changed after Hurricane Michael. My days were filled with long early-morning commutes and many hours of storm cleanup. My home, office and even one of my most sacred spaces – the altar in our sanctuary – had all been destroyed. I not only felt like God was far away; I felt like I could not find God. I wondered, 'Had God left and taken everything that felt safe in my life?'

One morning on my ride into town, I noticed a deer darting frantically from one downed tree to another. It looked scared and lost and seemed to be searching for something. Tears filled my eyes as I remembered Psalm 42:1. Like that deer, I was darting back and forth – desperately searching for God. With everything familiar and routine gone, it felt like God was gone too. But I just needed to look for God in new ways. I knew then that Hurricane Michael could take many things, but it could never take away God's presence.

Later that day I felt overwhelmed by the massive trees that had fallen in my yard, so I prayed. A few hours later, a group of volunteers offered to clear the trees. God had once again shown up in an unexpected way. I found God's presence as soon as I slowed down and looked.

Prayer: *Dear God, when we feel overwhelmed and lost, help us not to give up seeking your presence. Give us clear eyes to see you at work in ways we never expected. Amen*

Thought for the day: Even if all that feels safe and normal gets taken away, God will never leave me.

Heather Howell (Florida, USA)

Take every opportunity

Read 1 Corinthians 13:1–11

Lift up your eyes and look to the heavens: who created all these? He who brings out the starry host one by one and calls forth each of them by name. Because of his great power and mighty strength, not one of them is missing.
Isaiah 40:26 (NIV)

When I was a boy I would run along the railroad tracks and look up into the star-filled sky. I would jump with outstretched arms, shout, 'Up, up and away!' and wish to soar into the heavens like Superman among the bright stars. I wondered, 'Who created all the stars?' As I grew older, I came to know that God created the heavens and the earth and everything in it.

As a child, I admired Superman, but later in life I grew to admire a man that I observed at community and church functions. He would pick up others' empty plates and cups and carry them to the kitchen. He would help wash dishes, clean the tables and sweep the floors. If anyone needed anything, he would do his best to meet their need. I began to try to be more like him.

I put away my childish thoughts of being like Superman and started my adult life by taking every opportunity to serve people. I discovered that we do not need to look far to find opportunities to serve others and thus serve God.

Prayer: *Dear Father, help us to serve others through faith, hope and love. Always remind us that every act of service, no matter how small, is important to you. Amen*

Thought for the day: God will guide me to where I can be most helpful.

David D. Felty (Indiana, USA)

The big, living God

Read 1 Samuel 17:24–49

Who is this uncircumcised Philistine that he should defy the armies of the living God?
1 Samuel 17:26 (NRSV)

My sink and roof leaked last week. In addition to these problems, my spouse's business is suffering due to our country's uncertain political situation and economic downturn. Even with less income, we still have to pay the school fees for our biological and foster children. All together, these troubles feel big and insistent.

But God speaks to me through 1 Samuel 17:26. When all of Israel was afraid of Goliath, a giant Philistine warrior in impressive armour, David confidently decided to fight the champion soldier. Why was David so brave? Because he believed in the living God and that the people of God would not be overcome, even by Goliath.

While life can feel overwhelming, I am reminded that none of my problems is greater than my God. Through this scripture, God shows me that I have to stop saying, 'O God, I have a big problem!' Instead, like David, I can dare to say, 'Hi problem, I have a big God!'

Prayer: *Dear God, thank you for your lovingkindness that is new every morning. Help us to focus on you rather than the magnitude of the problems we face. Amen*

Thought for the day: Because my God is big, I can face anything.

Linda Chandra (Banten, Indonesia)

The night sky

Read Psalm 8:1–9

When I look at your heavens, the work of your fingers, the moon and the stars that you have established; what are human beings that you are mindful of them, mortals that you care for them?
Psalm 8:3–4 (NRSV)

It was too hot to sleep in my bedroom. After trying to find a comfortable position and sweating all the while, I went outside and laid a blanket on the small deck. I made myself comfortable and watched the stars. Before I moved to this rural area in Tennessee, where there is little light pollution and dark means dark, I went for weeks – even months – without looking up. I seldom saw the magnificence of the night sky. Where was my attention if not turned to the natural glory around me?

Looking at the stars, it doesn't take long for me to turn inward. As I look, I have two thoughts at once: Given the vastness of all that is, how is it that I exist? And, given that I am in the midst of this great vastness, how can my response be anything other than gratitude?

I pray that I can remain in the middle of those two thoughts, humble and grateful at the same time.

Prayer: *Lord of the universe, keep my attention turned upward so that I may find my place in this wondrous world you have created. Amen*

Thought for the day: I am wonderfully made in the image of God.

Doug Hagler (Tennessee, USA)

Small gestures

Read Matthew 5:13–16

Let your light shine before others, so that they may see your good works and give glory to your Father in heaven.
Matthew 5:16 (NRSV)

In my role as a career coach for high school students, I was presenting a lesson on the importance of a positive attitude in the workplace. A student I didn't know very well surprised me by noting my consistent positivity and asking where it came from. Without hesitation, I answered, 'Jesus!'

Through this experience, I realised that we have the opportunity to shine a light for the Lord in all situations. Our actions impact each person we encounter. As Christians, this is an opportunity to reflect God's light into what can be a dark world. This may seem daunting, but we are not alone. Jesus walks alongside us and inspires us.

Because of our relationship with Christ, we get to be his representatives and glorify God through our interactions with students, co-workers, customers, restaurant servers, sales associates and everyone else. Small gestures, like a smile or a friendly word, can open the door to share our faith with others. Who knows? We may be the only friendly face someone sees that day. And thanks to the love of our Savior, we always have a reason to smile and share the source of our joy with others.

Prayer: *Dear Jesus, thank you for loving us. Help us to glorify you by reflecting your love through our everyday interactions with others. Amen*

Thought for the day: My positive attitude can share the light of Christ with others.

Nikki Dyess (Alabama, USA)

Equipped

Read 2 Timothy 3:1–17

All Scripture is God-breathed and is useful for teaching, rebuking, correcting and training in righteousness, so that the servant of God may be thoroughly equipped for every good work.
2 Timothy 3:16–17 (NIV)

Years ago, our family embarked on a road trip through Africa. We travelled in a vehicle that was equipped for the rough, rural terrain, and we were well prepared with tools, extra fuel and supplies. We were confident that no matter what we faced, we had the necessary equipment to navigate our way safely. Throughout that trip we were exceedingly grateful for the hours of preparation we had invested in equipping ourselves. We constantly came across challenges that would have significantly delayed our progress or stopped our trip short had we not taken the time and effort to prepare.

In 2 Timothy 3:16–17, Paul lays out the importance of being prepared for the journey of life. To successfully navigate the changes and challenges we encounter, we must be well equipped. We can do this by investing wholeheartedly in the word of God. When we meditate on the Bible's wisdom, we will find that it fills our hearts and minds with truth, peace and strength. God's word equips us to handle any difficulty we might face. Scripture is our guide that will protect and carry us throughout our journey.

Prayer: *Dear God, thank you for the wisdom of your word. Equip us by your mercy to handle any challenge life may present. Amen*

Thought for the day: Meditating on the word of God will equip me for my life's journey.

Nelson Nwosu (Anambra, Nigeria)

Through the waves

Read Luke 8:4–15

These are the ones who, when they hear the word, hold it fast in an honest and good heart, and bear fruit with patient endurance.
Luke 8:15 (NRSV)

I was at the beach admiring God's beautiful creation. Wading into the water, I was being tossed around by rough ocean waves. I kept falling down and going under. It was quite funny, actually. I decided to go deeper in the water where the waves were easier to take and I wouldn't get knocked down.

I compared this experience to my relationship with God. When I grow deeper and closer to God, I can take on life's waves more easily. I don't get knocked down by every challenge that comes my way.

Deeper into the water, I could stand up and face the waves with boldness. When I dive deeper into scripture, God makes my burdens easier to carry. I'm learning every day to find the joy in the waves and allow God to carry the weight.

God waits for us to take the first step deeper into the waters. Sometimes our challenges may be too hard to take on by ourselves. But God is by our side wherever we go. We don't have to carry the weight alone.

Prayer: *Dear Lord, help us to grow closer to you and to release our burdens, trusting that you will help us carry them. Amen*

Thought for the day: As I draw nearer to God, my burdens become lighter.

Kaycee Reardon (West Virginia, USA)

PRAYER FOCUS: TO GROW CLOSER TO GOD

In all seasons

Read Psalm 92:12–15

In old age [the righteous] still produce fruit.
Psalm 92:14 (NRSV)

After years of walking the heart-wrenching path of dementia, our beloved mother passed away in her sleep. My brothers and I gathered in her room to weep, remember and pray. As we packed away her belongings, I picked up her well-worn Bible with *The Upper Room* tucked inside its tattered pages.

I turned to *The Upper Room* devotional for the day that Mum had died, and then to the Bible verses she had read just hours before her death. In her shaky handwriting, she had underlined the day's reading and had written *UR* and the date. Then she had penned, 'How True!' at the end of the passage. As I looked through her Bible, I found this pattern over and over: *UR*, the date and the words 'How True!' I sat and wept, sensing the presence of the Holy Spirit.

While her body and mind were failing, our mother continued her daily spiritual practice. Although she is gone, her powerful witness of God's faithfulness in every season of life will continue to speak to me and to many generations of our family. I am grateful for God's eternal promises.

Prayer: *Loving and eternal God, we praise you for the people who have taught us to walk in faith with confidence and with hope. May the love of Christ guide us in faithful living all our days. Amen*

Thought for the day: No matter the circumstance, God is faithful.

Karen Christy Kurtz (North Carolina, USA)

An unexpected answer

Read 1 Kings 19:1–13

Then [Elijah] lay down under the bush and fell asleep. All at once an angel touched him and said, 'Get up and eat.'
1 Kings 19:5 (NIV)

I had taken on too much and found myself physically and emotionally drained. Thoughts of all that I had committed to overwhelmed me. I flopped down on the couch and cried out to God, 'I don't know how to do it all. Right now I just want to give up. Please help me.' My eyes closed as I prayed and waited for an answer. An hour later I roused from slumber, upset with myself for falling asleep during prayer. I reflected on the situation and realised that when I called out in prayer, I didn't ask for specifics because I didn't know what I needed. But what I did ask for was help, and help came in the form of rest. An unexpected answer to prayer renewed my strength and focus.

The story of the prophet Elijah came to mind. He was exhausted and told God he'd had enough. Elijah was so discouraged by his circumstances that he asked God to take his life. Instead, God let him sleep and then sent an angel to give him something to eat. Strengthened, Elijah carried on and later was able to hear God's gentle whisper. Today God still provides rest to refresh us and renew our passion for trusting and obeying God.

Prayer: *Dear God, thank you for your love and provision. Thank you for always giving us what we need, even when we don't know what to ask for. Amen*

Thought for the day: God can renew my strength in unexpected ways.

Tandy Balson (Alberta, Canada)

'Show' versus 'sure'

Read Luke 18:9–14

As the body without the spirit is dead, so faith without deeds is dead.
James 2:26 (NIV)

In high school I outweighed my older brother Vincent by more than 35 pounds, worked out more often and could lift significantly more weight. I considered all of this to be an advantage. One afternoon we decided to wrestle in the yard. Despite my physical size, muscle tone and confidence, Vincent quickly beat me three times in a row. After his last victory he proclaimed, 'That's the difference between "show" muscles and "for-sure" muscles!'

Recently I was reminded of my brother's words while reflecting on a sermon about genuine faith: there is a faith that is just for show and a faith that is sure. The sure faith is based on obedience to God's word. A sure faith is developed through the disciplines of scripture study, prayer, worship and service.

Showy faith may look good, but just like my 'show' muscles, it is unable to withstand challenges or win even the smallest victory in life.

On the other hand, sure faith relies on the power and promises of God and helps us to stand when the floods come, lift burdens, spread hope and move mountains.

Prayer: *Help us, O God, to have a strong foundation and a sure faith. Amen*

Thought for the day: Sure faith is based on obedience to God.

Cassius Rhue (South Carolina, USA)

A change of direction

Read Psalm 92:1–5

The Lord will guide you always.
Isaiah 58:11 (NIV)

Most of my adult life has been spent in children's ministry. I first began as a volunteer in my church, then took a full-time position. I found no greater joy than seeing children's faces light up when they saw how God was working in their lives.

Then the day came when I couldn't continue this ministry because of staff changes in our church. I was heartbroken. I kept turning to God in prayer, asking what I should do – how I could best serve.

At about the same time, my mother was admitted to a nursing home for those with dementia. On one of my visits, we gathered for a music programme. I saw how the residents responded to the music, and I was amazed. I had played piano since childhood, and I volunteered to play each week. It was pure joy for me watching them sing along to songs they remembered from years ago. And it brought proud tears to my mother's eyes. After Mum died, I contacted some nursing homes nearer to where I live and offered to play music for the residents.

I never imagined that my gifts would lead me to serve outside of children's ministry. But these past few years have shown me that when we ask God for guidance, God leads us to places we may never have ventured.

Prayer: *Dear God, help us to let go of preconceived ideas so that we can hear your voice of wisdom for our lives. Amen*

Thought for the day: I will always find joy on the path God chooses for me.

Andrea Woronick (Connecticut, USA)

No longer a stranger

Read Ephesians 2:11–22

You are no longer strangers and aliens, but you are citizens with the saints and also members of the household of God.
Ephesians 2:19 (NRSV)

As a bright-eyed new Christian, I believed that everything in my life would suddenly be perfect and every problem would be resolved super-naturally. No one ever spoke about the process of change that needed to happen – the old ways of thinking that needed to change and the refining that God would do in me. In church I would look around at Christians who had been believers for many years. I would listen to their experiences of hearing the voice of the Holy Spirit and walking in God's will for their lives. I grew discouraged and felt like an outsider in a land that was not my own. I often wondered if I was even supposed to be a Christian, especially since I had once been a 'Gentile' and an 'unbeliever.'

Ephesians became my comfort and hope during those challenging times. Paul said that he was 'preaching among the Gentiles' in Ephesians 3:8, and I clung to Ephesians 2:19, which reminded me that I was no longer a stranger. I declared over and over that I was a citizen with the saints and a member of the household of God. And eventually the labels 'Gentile' and 'unbeliever' no longer defined me.

Prayer: *Dear God, thank you for welcoming us as members of your household. In Jesus' name. Amen*

Thought for the day: When I keep my focus on God, all labels fall away.

Teresa Naidoo (KwaZulu-Natal, South Africa)

The telephone tree

Read John 15:1–5

Jesus said, 'I am the vine; you are the branches. If you remain in me and I in you, you will bear much fruit; apart from me you can do nothing.'
John 15:5 (NIV)

As I write, many of us around the world are 'locked down' because of a pandemic. Many churches have cancelled worship services, Bible studies, Sunday school classes, committee meetings and mission projects.

At first, we were dismayed at the thought of closing our church campus. Our concerns were lessened when some of our members began live streaming our worship services and making recordings that could be viewed at any time. Our pastors created a telephone tree – a network of people who would contact others on a regular basis to support each other, worship together by phone, share joys and sorrows and pray together. Others reached out by email or private messages through social media. The network spread wider and was transformed into something new.

When the current health crisis has abated and our church can resume its regular activities, our congregation plans to continue its new ways of ministering to our neighbours, friends, those who are homebound and others. Today's reading reminds us that Jesus is the vine that connects us to one another and to God. Jesus is with us no matter how we connect.

Prayer: *Gracious and loving God, thank you for providing us with creative ways to follow you and the reminder that church is not a building but a community of your faithful followers. In Jesus' name we pray. Amen*

Thought for the day: There are many ways to connect to God and to one another.

Doug Wingert (Arizona, USA)

God's garden

Read Psalm 104:27–35

Jesus said, 'My Father is glorified by this, that you bear much fruit and become my disciples.'
John 15:8 (NRSV)

This year my husband and I decided to turn our little-used back deck into a container garden. It is working beautifully. I am overjoyed by the brilliant colours of the flowers, the fragrance of the herbs and the lush green of the vegetables. Each plant is beautiful on its own, but together they display the beauty of God's handiwork. I have found great pleasure in tending this new garden and learning what each plant needs. Some need more water than others, some need more space to spread out, all need regular fertilising for nourishment and all need occasional pruning.

As I work in my garden, I think of how God cares for each of us. God gives us space to grow and provides living water to keep us vibrant, and God nourishes us with scripture and prunes us when necessary so we can grow and be more fruitful. God knows just what we need. We each are beautiful in our own way, but together we are truly God's garden.

Prayer: *Dear God, thank you for the loving care you provide each and every day. Help us to grow and bloom as your disciples wherever we are planted. Amen*

Thought for the day: God's loving care and provision make my life more fruitful.

Jane Rager (Virginia, USA)

Dry bones

Read Ezekiel 37:1–14

The Lord God proclaims to these bones: I am about to put breath in you, and you will live again.
Ezekiel 37:5 (CEB)

During a recent battle with depression, I found myself devoid of all desire for God. For a few months, I lived in a seemingly impenetrable fog. Morning devotions were a struggle, church sermons felt wearisome and ministry was a burden too great to bear. It was a dry season unlike anything I had ever experienced. At the lowest points of my journey, I railed at God, 'How could you let this happen to me again?'

One day, I was seized by a once-familiar desire to open my Bible, and the Holy Spirit led me to the book of Ezekiel. 'Mortal, can these bones live?' When I read these words, I immediately felt a kinship with Ezekiel. I was pondering the dry bones of my life and wondering if they could ever come alive again. I too was crying out, 'My bones are dry, my hope is lost, I myself am cut off!'

I continued to read about how as Ezekiel prophesied there was a rattling sound as the bones came together. Eventually, breath entered them; they came to life and stood up on their feet. I could not stop my tears. As I savoured this story, God breathed fresh life into me. Hope that I thought I had lost started to blossom again out of the words of scripture. I was reassured that God had never left my side. Even when hope seems lost, God knows our struggles and can breathe new life into us.

Prayer: *Dear God, speak to us in the valley and make our dry bones come alive again with your breath of life. Amen*

Thought for the day: As we go through times of spiritual drought, let us wait for God to breathe life into us.

Piyumi Kapugeekiyana (Western Province, Sri Lanka)

Life's hurdles

Read Isaiah 40:28–31

Since we are surrounded by so great a cloud of witnesses, let us also lay aside every weight and the sin that clings so closely, and let us run with perseverance the race that is set before us.
Hebrews 12:1 (NRSV)

My high school track team had two hurdlers: one was graceful and fluid, hardly ever tipping over a hurdle; the other hit and tipped over many of the hurdles as he ran. The not-so-graceful hurdler was the faster of the two.

Even though I was not a hurdler, I had my own obstacles to overcome as a miler on the track team. Because of some physical limitations, I often finished well behind the top finishers in competitions, but it was not for lack of desire or preparation. I never gave up and always finished every race.

In life, we face many hurdles and challenges. Many seem insurmountable. We may not want to face these difficulties, and we may want to give up. But with God's help, we can gain the strength to overcome any obstacle – even those we face every day. When we share our concerns, God will show us the way. All God asks us to do is to run the race set before us with faith in God's ways.

Prayer: *God of all strength and compassion, help us to seek you in times of need so that we may continue to run the race you have set before us. Amen*

Thought for the day: God will help me over every hurdle.

Jim Seymour (New York, USA)

The language of prayer

Read Ephesians 6:18–20

The Lord says, 'Then you will call on me and come and pray to me, and I will listen to you.'
Jeremiah 29:12 (NIV)

While attending university, I lived in the international house. What an amazing opportunity to meet new people, learn about cultures other than my own and try different foods! But one roommate gave me an even greater gift; she showed me God's language of prayer.

Magguy and I connected the moment we met. Her easy laugh, bright smile and love for Jesus matched my own. From the Democratic Republic of the Congo, Magguy knew at least five languages before coming to the United States. However, she did not feel confident about her English skills. She asked me to help her with English reading and comprehension. So we began a new daily ritual using *The Upper Room*.

Magguy read the scripture and devotional aloud. Then, I would ask her questions about what the author had written. After practising her English we would pray together. Magguy prayed in a mixture of her native tongues, while I prayed in English. I may not have understood her words, but I began to learn God's deeper language of prayer. God speaks in silence, emotion, thought, longing, praise, lament, joy, gratitude. Praying together led to a season of prayer growth for me as both my world and my understanding of God's language grew.

Prayer: *Holy Jesus, we trust that you hear us as we pray in our many languages. Enrich our hearts as we listen for your response. Amen*

Thought for the day: The language of prayer can unite us.

Michelle L. Knight (Indiana, USA)

The colours of life

Read Genesis 9:12–17

I have set my rainbow in the clouds, and it will be the sign of the covenant between me and the earth.
Genesis 9:13 (NIV)

After a heavy rain shower began to slacken, sunshine and blue sky peeked through the clouds that remained. Then I saw an arc of brilliant colors – a rainbow shining against the dark clouds.

In the book of Genesis, a great flood covered the earth. Only Noah, his family and all kinds of animals were saved in an ark that Noah built following God's command. When the flood abated, a rainbow appeared as a sign of God's mercy in preserving life on earth.

The clouds of bereavement, illness, depression or loneliness can darken our lives. We may feel far from God's love. Just as rainbows shine in contrast to the dark clouds, perhaps God's promises to us become more real when life's clouds overshadow us. Even – perhaps especially – in our difficult times, God is with us and will bring the colours of joy and hope back to our lives in surprising ways.

Prayer: *Dear Lord, be with us this day whatever our circumstances as we watch for signs of your love and mercy. Amen*

Thought for the day: I will remember God's promise in the rainbow.

Anne Rasmussen (England, United Kingdom)

When you don't fit in

Read John 14:1–7

In my Father's house there are many dwelling places. If it were not so, would I have told you that I go to prepare a place for you? And If I go and prepare a place for you, I will come again and will take you to myself, so that where I am, there you may be also.
John 14:2–3 (NRSV)

When I stepped into my office building one dreary Thursday, I was met by my boss, who asked me to sit down. A tense five minutes later, I learnt that it was my last day working for the organisation after more than 25 years of service. A restructuring was underway, she said, and I didn't fit in the plans for the future. Fighting tears, I was deeply wounded. In that instant, I questioned my life's worth. 'How would I ever recover?', I thought.

After the shock and anger of rejection gave way to clarity, a deeper truth emerged. In this world, we will face rejection or be told that we don't fit in. But I know that I always have a place in God's future – in God's plans. God's kingdom will never be restructured, downsized, streamlined or whatever other euphemism that says, 'You just don't fit in.' God will always have a place for me.

Through God's grace, we belong. Our place in the kingdom to come is waiting for us, just as Jesus said it would be. I can think of nothing more comforting than knowing – without a doubt – that in God's kingdom, both on earth and in heaven, we fit in.

Prayer: *Father God, regardless of what life deals us, thank you for your assurance and the comfort of knowing we have a place with you – both here and in the kingdom yet to come. Amen*

Thought for the day: Because of God's grace, I always fit in.

D. Gerow Baker (Oklahoma, USA)

A genuine faith

Read Psalm 139:13–24

Search me, O God, and know my heart; test me and know my thoughts.
Psalm 139:23 (NRSV)

The CT technician stepped from behind the glass partition. As I sat up to leave, she approached me with a few questions: 'You have clips in your chest from open-heart surgery?' 'Yes,' I replied. 'And you have had a total hip replacement?' Again, I answered yes. Finally she asked, 'And you have a permanent colostomy?' 'Well, yes, I do.' She looked shocked and blurted out, 'But you look so good on the outside!'

I have laughed over this story many times in retelling it to my family. I may appear outwardly healthy, but inwardly I have signs of past surgeries and illnesses. As the technician saw me, I looked well, whole and strong. My outer appearance did not show what my inner body would reveal.

As I considered this conversation again, I felt a strong conviction. I might appear to be spiritually healthy, strong in my faith and obedient to God. But God is the only one who knows my heart, my thoughts and my desires. And I want what God sees and knows about me to match up with what I present to the world.

Prayer: *Dear Lord, search our hearts. Show us how to align our hearts and our actions so that others may know we follow you. Amen*

Thought for the day: God knows my heart, thoughts and desires.

Linda M. Harris (Virginia, USA)

Problems – or opportunities?

Read Colossians 3:12–14

Moreover, we have all had human fathers who disciplined us and we respected them for it. How much more should we submit to the Father of spirits and live!

Hebrews 12:9 (NIV)

During lockdown I set myself the task of learning to touch-type using an online typing course. It has been interesting to see my speed and accuracy improve with daily practice. While the programme gives plenty of good teaching and passages to type to improve my standard, it also monitors the keys I repeatedly get wrong – 'problem letters' – and it will, if chosen, give extra practice in those ones. It's not pleasurable to do this, as whenever these letters come up I automatically tense up. But with frequent repetition, they don't seem so scary.

In our lives, God sees areas that need improvement. Are we impatient? God sends us people who will try our patience. Are we grudging in our giving? He will give us opportunities to be generous. Are we fearful? God will teach us by life's experiences to depend on him and trust him more. These lessons are not pleasurable either, but they are so necessary, and we are wise to heed them.

Prayer: *Father, you know what is best for us, even if it seems tough. We know that you have promised never to give us more than we can handle with your Spirit's help and guidance. Amen*

Thought for the day: Problems can become opportunities to lean more on God's faithfulness.

Christine Hay (Scotland, United Kingdom)

Intentionally made

Read Romans 12:4–8

I praise you, for I am fearfully and wonderfully made. Wonderful are your works; that I know very well.
Psalm 139:14 (NRSV)

I was a very reserved child – always the last to talk in a group, make new friends or start a conversation. Although I knew what I wanted to say, I had difficulty expressing myself. I was displeased with God for making me this way. I wanted to be more outspoken, but that was not who I was created to be.

I did not appreciate my personality until I found myself leaning towards working in ministry. As a youth pastor, I need to listen to and consider carefully the stories and situations that people bring to me for counsel. I finally understood the value and the reason for the personality God gave me. It helps me to discern the truth, make accurate deductions and give wise counsel. Being swift to listen and slow to speak has equipped me well for my calling.

God knows our future and has prepared us for it by giving us the abilities and personalities that best suit our purpose and calling. We may be different from those we admire, but we cannot be who we are not. We can accept, appreciate and celebrate who we are – unique individuals, intentionally made for God's purpose.

Prayer: *Dear Lord, help us to see ourselves as you see us, and to appreciate who you have made us to be. Amen*

Thought for the day: Today I will celebrate how God made me and use my skills for God's glory.

Muyiwa Benralph Olaiya (Federal Capital Territory, Nigeria)

Casting nets

Read Luke 5:1–11

Simon answered, 'Master, we've worked hard all night and haven't caught anything. But because you say so, I will let down the nets.'
Luke 5:5 (NIV)

As a career fisherman, Simon – also called Peter – was an expert. Yet, here was this stranger offering instructions from the shore. I imagine Simon and his crew tried to say no respectfully. Maybe he brought out all the excuses: they had just worked the best fishing hours with no results; their nets were washed, mended and put away; they were ready for a break. Basically, now was not the time. But when they finally followed Jesus' advice, their boat almost sank with the weight of their catch.

I am a lot like Peter. I consider myself an expert in knowing the best time to share the gospel. I have lots of excuses when Jesus calls: I am not articulate; I may not know the right answer; I could look foolish or be mocked. But then I remember that it is the Holy Spirit who leads people to Christ. All I have to do is be faithful to the commission Christ gives me and simply throw out the nets. Jesus is with me and tells me, 'Do not be afraid.'

Prayer: *Guide us, Holy Spirit, that we may hear the call and to be faithful in casting our nets, even when we feel inadequate. Amen*

Thought for the day: The Holy Spirit transforms hearts when I share Jesus' story.

Rhonda Douglas (Texas, USA)

Follow Christ

Read John 21:20–23

Jesus answered, 'If I want him to remain alive until I return, what is that to you? You must follow me.'
John 21:22 (NIV)

When I was young, my sisters and I would sometimes tell on one another. Typically, it would be over a minor infraction or an annoying behaviour. My mum or grandmother would respond to the telltale, 'You just worry about yourself.' My primary school teachers would say something similar to students exhibiting the same type of behaviour.

When I became a Christian, I realised – much to my dismay – that I often reverted to my habit of telling on others even though I was older and felt I had matured. I may not have vocalised it, the way I did when I was a child, but in my mind I would judge those I felt had wronged me or my loved ones. I thought that as a Christian I had the right to pass judgement on others.

Then I read today's scripture passage. It reminded me of the words of my mum and grandmother all those years ago – except now they came from the Lord. Today, when I believe someone has done something wrong and I mentally tell on them, I hear Jesus say, 'What is that to you? You must follow me.'

Prayer: *Gracious God, thank you for the wisdom you shared with us through your Son. Help us to follow him to glorify your holy name. In his name we pray. Amen*

Thought for the day: I am called to follow Christ.

Chad Radune (Ohio, USA)

Growing up

While on a retreat I was paired for conversation with a delightful man full of grace and wisdom. I later learnt that he was an influential member of a political group I had all but cursed earlier in the week. At first, I was sad and conflicted. How could we really be friends, given our differences? The next morning in prayer, as I wrestled with the Lord over what to do, I heard, 'Grow up, Stephen. Grow in my love.'

After all these years as a follower of Jesus, I am still learning what it means to grow in Christ. Dallas Willard described growing in Christ as a 'golden triangle of spiritual transformation'. By embracing our situation, opening our lives to the guidance of the Spirit and practising spiritual disciplines, we continually 'take off the old human nature with its practices and put on the new nature' (Colossians 3:9–10, CEB) of a life lived in the likeness and integrity of Christ. All three sides of the triangle are essential to the process of transformation.

On the first side of the triangle we embrace our situation. Through the hard knocks of life, God can challenge our self-sufficiency and stretch our ability to empathise with the suffering of others. We are not embracing the situation when we blame other people's wrongheadedness or immaturity for our troubles or trials. Jesus could have grumbled that life was unfair to him, complained that sinful people were unworthy of him or asked God for a loftier, less humiliating assignment. Instead, as Paul reminds us, '[Jesus] emptied himself... becoming obedient to the point of death, even death on a cross' (Philippians 2:7–8). And James wrote: 'My brothers and sisters, think of the various tests you encounter as occasions for joy. After all, you know that the testing of your faith produces endurance. Let this endurance complete its work so that you may be fully mature, complete, and lacking in nothing' (James 1:2–4).

On the second side, we open our lives to the guidance of the Spirit. Jesus knew that we would need a helper as we strive to live a Christlike life. When he departed, he gave us the Spirit, the same helper that had helped him (John 14:25–26). At his baptism, the Holy Spirit descended upon Jesus like a dove (Luke 3:2–22). When launching his ministry, Jesus acknowledged the Spirit as the source of the courage and guidance he would need daily to respond in God-like ways to the people he encountered (Luke 4:2–22). An Upper Room prayer that helps me start my day begins, 'New every morning is your love, great God of light, and all day long you are working for good in the world.' The simple reminder that God is already at work among us stirs in me an openness to participate in what God is doing in the world.

The third side of the triangle reminds us to practise spiritual disciplines. Spiritual disciplines are the ways we imitate Christ, share in his life and make ourselves available to the Spirit for the transformation of our hearts and minds — especially in the areas of our lives where we are self-absorbed. By meditating on scripture, we open our narrow minds to the mind of Christ. Through prayer, we open our little hearts to the big heartedness of Christ. When we serve our neighbours in need, we open our fists to the hands of Christ and join in the work of mending the world God loves. With these and other spiritual disciplines, we 'put on the Lord Jesus Christ' (Romans 13:14, NRSV) and day by day — guided by the Spirit — we grow in Christ's likeness.

QUESTIONS FOR REFLECTION

1 When has an encounter with the Lord or some other life event challenged you to grow up? How did you respond to that challenge?

2 Which side of the transformation triangle is most natural for you? Which needs more practice as you grow in Christlikeness?

Stephen D. Bryant, former publisher and world editor

A guiding hand

Read Psalm 28:1–9

The Lord is my strength and my shield; my heart trusts in him, and he helps me.
Psalm 28:7 (NIV)

Twice a week I wait for a morning bus at the top of a small hill. While I wait, I watch as primary-school children ride bikes to school with their parents. The children often struggle to get up the hill on their bikes, but their loving parents give a word of encouragement or lean down from their own bikes to gently guide their child up the hill. Watching these parents makes me think of the guiding hand of God in my life.

In my early 20s, after completing my master's degree, I went to training college in Auckland, New Zealand, with the intention of becoming a high school teacher. While there I was unexpectedly offered a lecturing job at an Australian university. I prayed for guidance in this dilemma.

On the Sunday before I was to give my answer, I was teaching a Bible class at church when God's guidance came to me clearly. This was where I should be – teaching teenagers, not working in a university. Like a good parent, God helped me recognise my strengths, and I went on to have a rewarding career as a teacher. Confiding in God in prayer, seeking guidance and receiving answers have been mainstays in my life. Looking back, I can see that God has always been with me.

Prayer: *Loving God, thank you for always being with us. Grant us the faith to trust in your guidance and help us to recognise your hand at work in our lives. Amen*

Thought for the day: God will help me recognise my strengths.

Margaret Martin (Australian Capital Territory, Australia)

Spring flowers

Read Song of Songs 2:10–13

Forget the former things; do not dwell on the past. See, I am doing a new thing! Now it springs up; do you not perceive it? I am making a way in the wilderness and streams in the wasteland.

Isaiah 43:18–19 (NIV)

One spring day many years ago, I went to church to have a talk with Jesus. Getting out of my car, I passed a flower bed overcome with weeds. This sight made me angry. I did a lot of work for my church, and I couldn't believe that others would ignore the weeds and just assume that I would take care of them.

I went into the building and got sidetracked. As I came out, I passed the weeds and got angry again. This reminded me of the whole purpose of my visit. I had forgotten to talk with Jesus! Going back in, I spent time with my Lord at the altar. Coming back out, I no longer noticed the weeds but the beautiful purple violets.

This made me think about how many times I overlook God's handiwork. It happens so easily. Spending time with God in light of my anger and troubles reminded me of how Jesus is like the spring. Just as we see flowers and trees and other vegetation flourishing in the sunlight, our relationship with Jesus can help us to bloom. When we are fed by him, the world looks more beautiful.

Prayer: *Dear Lord Jesus, open up our eyes and hearts to the newness we can experience as we walk with you. Amen*

Thought for the day: When I get frustrated by the weeds of life, I will look for God's flowers.

Jerrie Green (West Virginia, USA)

A change in pattern

Read Psalm 103:1–5

We take captive every thought to make it obedient to Christ.
2 Corinthians 10:5 (NIV)

One day as I washed dishes, I agonised over things I had said in an earlier conversation. I combed over my words: Why did I say that? I should have thought more carefully before I spoke. I pictured myself reliving the conversation and saying different words.

Then God spoke to my heart. I stopped berating myself and started to focus on worshipping God: 'Praise you, God, for you are my creator. Praise you, for you are my saviour. Praise you, for you are my sustainer.'

When I finished my prayer of praise, I paused to contemplate what had happened. Earlier, when I was focusing on my shortcomings, I felt overwhelmed and exhausted. But when I switched my thoughts to praise God, I felt exhilarated and energetic.

This practice of redirecting my thoughts from beating myself down to praising God taught me that our creator gives us the ability to change our thinking. We can change the pattern of our thoughts from focusing on ourselves to focusing on the Almighty. With this mindset we can live faithfully.

Prayer: *Dear God, thank you for showing us the ways you want us to live – in our thoughts, our words and our deeds. Amen*

Thought for the day: Praising God can renew my spirit and give me strength.

Delores Kight (Florida, USA)

Navigation

Read Psalm 119:105–112

I will never forget your precepts, for by them you have preserved my life.
Psalm 119:93 (NIV)

I will never forget my first experience using a car navigation system more than 15 years ago.

My daughter's wedding was to be held in a big city about 200 miles away. I had never been to that city, and I decided to install a vehicle navigation system for the drive. As my wife and I travelled, the landscape changed and gradually the scenery became unfamiliar. I checked the monitor often and followed the system's directions. Then at last, the destination appeared on the screen and to my surprise we had arrived.

This amazing experience reminds me of our Christian life. Our final destination has been set to God's kingdom, and we are now in the midst of driving on the road of life, looking to the Bible for guidance as we go. It is inevitable that we will face difficulties, hardships and temptations. However, if we carefully follow God's guidance in scripture, our final destination will be guaranteed.

Prayer: *Help us, O God, to study scripture carefully so that we can remain on the road that leads to you. We pray as Jesus taught us, 'Our Father which art in heaven, Hallowed be thy name. Thy kingdom come. Thy will be done in earth, as it is in heaven. Give us this day our daily bread. And forgive us our debts, as we forgive our debtors. And lead us not into temptation, but deliver us from evil: For thine is the kingdom, and the power, and the glory, for ever.'* Amen*

Thought for the day: God's guidance is always trustworthy.

Kazuo Ishikawa (Akita, Japan)

PRAYER FOCUS: FOR STRENGTH TO OBEY GOD'S WORD
*Matthew 6:9–13 (KJV)

Offering help

Read Matthew 5:38–42

Give to the one who asks you, and do not turn away from the one who wants to borrow from you.
Matthew 5:42 (NIV)

My boyfriend and I were approached in a grocery store parking lot by a man we assumed to be homeless. He asked politely if we had a dollar to spare, as he wanted to buy tacos from a nearby fast-food restaurant. My boyfriend quickly got out his wallet and gave the man $20. The man initially refused, but my boyfriend explained, 'I know it's a rough world out here; anything can help.' When the man finally accepted and gave us permission to pray with him, we prayed for his protection and Christ's continued care for him. My boyfriend and I watched the man cross the street and enter the restaurant. Once in the car, I asked my boyfriend what compelled him to be so generous. He said simply, 'I felt God tugging at my heart to help him.'

Charity is one of the many virtues that Christ asks us to practise daily. Any act, whether giving to someone in need or just spending time with a lonely person, glorifies Christ and is an outward expression of his love. When we trust and act on the 'heart tugs,' we can change the outcome of someone's day. We don't know the impact we may have on others.

Prayer: *Loving God, grant us the courage to help others in any way we can. May we glorify you and show your love through acts of charity. Amen*

Thought for the day: Even one generous act can inspire change in our world.

Becca Stiegelmar (Texas, USA)

Inheritance

Read Psalm 145:1–13

One generation commends your works to another; they tell of your mighty acts.
Psalm 145:4 (NIV)

My mother's book of family history depicted how her parents survived the Russian Revolution of 1917. Then, religious persecution forced them and many other Christians to flee across Europe. They were often hungry, exhausted, cold and afraid. Grief seemed to follow Grandma and Grandpa: six of their 13 children died very young; many relatives were imprisoned in Siberia; Grandpa died in his 50s; and Grandma watched my mother walk away from her faith. But Grandma never lost her faith. Even when she did not get to witness the impact of her devotion, she trusted God. In one handwritten page in the family record book, Grandma begged her children and grandchildren to love God and follow Christ.

During devastating trials, King David experienced God's steadfast love and faithfulness. Psalm 145 reflects his love, trust and reverence for God. His words encourage future generations to remain hopeful.

Grandma's faith through suffering reflected her trust in an all-powerful God. She left a legacy of hope that I have turned to in my own battles with grief, fear and exhaustion. Through this inheritance from my grandmother, God has increased my faith.

Prayer: *Dear Lord, thank you for those who have left faithful legacies. Help us to live faithfully for the sake of future generations. Amen*

Thought for the day: My faithful living can make a difference for future generations.

Candice Lucey (British Columbia, Canada)

Ambassadors for Christ

Read 2 Corinthians 5:16–21

We are ambassadors for Christ, since God is making his appeal through us; we entreat you on behalf of Christ, be reconciled to God.
2 Corinthians 5:20 (NRSV)

Ambassadors appointed by their governments are stationed in countries all across the world as representatives of their nations. As spokespeople and envoys to other governments, ambassadors carry influence and communicate the policies of their countries.

Christ calls his followers to be ambassadors – to represent him before all people. As ambassadors of Christ, we are to reflect Christ's love, mercy, grace, compassion, joy and generosity. What an awesome responsibility it is to represent Christ!

As ambassadors of Christ, we are charged with bearing the likeness of Christ to the world. What we say and do, and how we respond to others will be a strong witness to the kingdom of God that Christ revealed.

The apostle Paul tells us that we have been appointed and confirmed by Christ to be his ambassadors. We can fulfil this calling when we centre our lives on Christ's love and forgiveness.

Prayer: *Dear God, forgive us when we fail to represent you well, and strengthen us with your never-ending love and grace to renew our commitment to you. Amen*

Thought for the day: I represent Christ when I live out his love.

Todd Diedrich (Wisconsin, USA)

A change of focus

Read Acts 1:4–8
Go and make disciples of all nations, baptising them in the name of the Father and of the Son and of the Holy Spirit.
Matthew 28:19 (NIV)

While I was in medical school, I attended church regularly, but my room-mate did not know much about God. However, she became interested in the Bible I kept by my bedside table. When I would spend time deeply focused on my coursework, she would ask me about Jesus and the Christian way of life. It annoyed me to have to stop what I was doing and respond to her, but the interruptions compelled me to more actively share my faith.

Then I read Luke 24:46–47, where Jesus, as he was about to leave the earth, said: 'The Messiah will suffer and rise… and repentance for the forgiveness of sins will be preached in his name to all nations.' I realised then that I had not understood God's full purpose for my life. Studying medicine was not my only goal. As a follower of Christ, I was also called to preach and share the good news of the gospel.

After further reflection, I began to speak with my roommate about Jesus Christ and his teachings. After a while she became a faithful disciple of Jesus. Encouraged by Christ's teachings in scripture, I am glad I listened and accepted God's prompting 'to go and make disciples'.

Prayer: *Interrupt us, O God, when our focus needs to shift. Inspire us to be ready to share your good news. In the name of Jesus. Amen*

Thought for the day: How is God shifting the focus of my life?

Lillian Saldaña Campos (La Habana, Cuba)

Following the call

Read John 10:25–29

My sheep listen to my voice; I know them, and they follow me.
John 10:27 (NIV)

Wood ducks build their nests in hollow, rotted tree cavities, which are sometimes up to 60 feet above the ground. Within a day of hatching, the ducklings climb out of their nests. Following their mother's beckoning call, they leap from the safety and comfort of the nest and fall to the ground below before making their way to water where their mother awaits. The ducklings do not hesitate to follow the voice they know and trust. They make this jump before they have learned to fly; yet they trust the call to come.

After discovering the fascinating beginnings of a wood duck's life, I began to wonder how much I trust the voice of the One who cares for me. Am I willing to leave all that is safe and familiar and follow the shepherd's call, even if that means leaping into the great unknown?

The ducklings' obedience is natural and instinctive. They show no fear – only trust. What a strong reminder to focus on the shepherd's voice with full assurance of his loving guidance!

Prayer: *Dear Lord, help us to follow you, trusting in your care for us. Amen*

Thought for the day: I can always trust the voice of my shepherd.

Jessica E. Dutton (Maine, USA)

Offering what we have

Read Psalm 118:21–25

The stone that the builders rejected has become the chief cornerstone.
Psalm 118:22 (NRSV)

My old wheelbarrow had rusted out, and both handles had been broken, repaired and re-broken. I was about to throw it in a dumpster with no regret. But then a person next to me said, 'Your wheelbarrow has a good wheel. Can I have it?' He had brought his wheelbarrow to the dump because its wheel had broken, but with my good wheel he could repair his wheelbarrow. I was delighted that someone could benefit from this object I was about to throw away.

Sometimes we see no value left in something we choose to discard. It is a happy surprise when someone tells us that what we have is just what they need. Similarly, we can look at our lives and think we have nothing useful left to give, especially when our bodies and minds stop working like they used to. But we may discover new ways to help a person in need or make someone's day with kind words. What we believe holds no value may be what matters most to someone else. When I am discouraged by my mistakes, I try to remember that sometimes by offering the things we may overlook or devalue we can become blessings to others. God can use what we reject to change the world.

Prayer: *Gracious God, may your Spirit flow through those parts of us that we have given up on. Help us to look for the blessings in others that they may not see. Amen*

Thought for the day: What I reject, God may use for good.

Jonathan Scott (Connecticut, USA)

Called by name

Read Isaiah 43:1–3

Do not fear, for I have redeemed you; I have called you by name, you are mine.
Isaiah 43:1 (NRSV)

Some years ago, I accompanied a group of school students on a trip to the World War I battlefields in Belgium. We walked through trenches imagining what it was like to be knee-deep in mud. We looked across a sea of white headstones in a beautifully kept British cemetery. We heard the last post and kept two minutes silence at the Menin Gate in Ypres. I remembered my great-uncle who had died at the Battle of the Somme in 1916. The students shared their family stories.

Now we were at Langemark, a German cemetery where over 44,000 young men were buried; 25,000 of these were in a mass grave about the size of a tennis court. There were no headstones; just grave markers laid flat on the cold earth. Most of the soldiers had no name to mark their last resting place. It was a bleak autumn day with oak leaves thick upon the ground.

I knelt beside the communal grave and brushed the leaves from the inscription: *Ich habe dich bei deine Name gerufen. Du bist mein.* ('I have called you by your name. You are mine.')

I no longer thought of an anonymous enemy but only of young men, little older than those in our group, known by name and loved by God.

Prayer: *Lord of all, may we love our enemies and pray for those who persecute us, for Jesus' sake. Amen*

Thought for the day: God's love extends beyond human boundaries.

Andrew Dutton (England, United Kingdom)

No matter the distance

Read Matthew 8:5–13

The centurion replied, 'Lord, I do not deserve to have you come under my roof. But just say the word, and my servant will be healed.'
Matthew 8:8 (NIV)

The phone rang, and it was too early for good news. Still half-asleep, I answered the call from my parents. My sister Mary had been in a car accident, and they were en route to the hospital. She had suffered a traumatic brain injury and was in a coma. They said they would know more if she survived the first 24 hours.

For the rest of the day, I prayed and wept and screamed in my bedroom. Because I was overseas at the time, it was true agony to be so far away and know my sister was on the verge of death. Eventually, in an attempt to find some comfort, I read today's scripture.

The centurion was not physically near to his suffering servant. Yet, Jesus healed the servant without being in the servant's presence. I took comfort in that story, knowing that distance is irrelevant to God.

My sister lived, but she still suffers the effects of her injuries and resides at home with my parents. I still live far away and cannot be there as much as I would like. But I take heart knowing that our faith overcomes earthly separation. Geographic distance cannot isolate us from our loved ones in need, nor the love, healing and protection of our Lord Jesus Christ.

Prayer: *Dear heavenly Father, help us to have the faith to know that you hear our prayers, no matter the time or distance. Watch over our loved ones who are suffering. Amen*

Thought for the day: No distance can separate me from God.

Johnny Nelson (Texas, USA)

Unconditional love

Read Hosea 11:1–8

When Israel was a child, I loved him… How can I give you up, Ephraim? How can I hand you over, Israel?
Hosea 11:1, 8 (NIV)

My husband and I have five children. Raising them brought quite a few challenges. One son in particular went through a very difficult period from the age of 15 into adulthood. We experienced many sleepless nights, tears, anger and just plain weariness during those years.

Israel, too, constantly tried God's patience by worshipping false gods and turning their backs on God. Hosea writes that Israel's unfaithfulness resulted in foreign powers conquering their government and exiling their people into distant lands. However, God never stopped loving them: they were children of the Almighty.

Through God's grace, we also never gave up on our son. We loved him and prayed for him through his many angry years. Today he is a hardworking young man and the father of three delightful children of his own.

As Israel's parent, God's love and compassion were all-encompassing. And just as God never gave up on the people of Israel, the Lord never gives up on us.

Prayer: *Dear Father, thank you for your unconditional love that spills over into our lives and hearts. Give us the courage to love others even when it is difficult. Amen*

Thought for the day: Because God faithfully loves me, I will faithfully love others.

Dianne Fegan (Queensland, Australia)

God healed my heart

Read Matthew 9:18–22

The righteous cry out, and the Lord hears them; he delivers them from all their troubles. The Lord is close to the brokenhearted and saves those who are crushed in spirit.
Psalm 34:17–18 (NIV)

My left knee throbbed, the spot between my shoulder blades ached and my thumb joints screamed at me. Arthritis and fibromyalgia were causing me great pain. For a while I was angry because I could no longer embroider, something I had enjoyed for years. My hands would ache if I quilted or sewed by hand for any length of time.

As all these changes to my body were taking place, my heart broke. I cried out to God with the typical question, 'Why?' I felt sorry for myself. But then I felt the Holy Spirit's nudge to pray for healing. The healing wasn't for my body; it was for my attitude. So I prayed and asked God for comfort and peace with my situation. Without hesitation, God poured grace over me.

I still struggle sometimes. When I do, I bow my head and seek my Father, who loves me. God continues to heal my crushed spirit, and I praise God for being with me always.

Thought for the day: God hears and answers my prayers.

Prayer: *Dear God, heal those who are broken, both physically and spiritually. Give us all new days and new ways to find the joy in our lives. Amen*

Penny Frost McGinnis (Ohio, USA)

Ray of hope

Read Habakkuk 3:17–19

He has made everything beautiful in its time. He has also set eternity in the human heart; yet no one can fathom what God has done from beginning to end.
Ecclesiastes 3:11 (NIV)

I looked out of the window. It was a cold, grey and rainy morning in late autumn. The leaves had fallen from the trees, winter was fast approaching and the whole country was facing strict quarantine measures due to the Covid-19 virus. I was thinking of the week ahead, not just for myself, but for church friends, family and people known to me, several in other countries. I was praying for God to walk beside us all and to give us peace and direction for everything we had to face in life. My mood reflected the weather that I could see from the window.

I was reading Habakkuk, and as I came to 3:17–19, the rain temporarily stopped, a gap in the clouds appeared and a bright ray of sunshine illuminated the room in which I was sitting, bringing a warmth to the cold air. I then recalled the words from Ecclesiastes quoted above, and was reminded that God is in control of his creation. Even in difficult times, he does walk beside us.

As I finished my morning Bible study and prayer time, my mood had changed. I felt encouraged to face the day with renewed hope about the difficult things being faced at this time by so many people around the world.

Prayer: *Dear Lord, thank you for many reminders in scripture, and in creation, that you are with us throughout each day. Amen*

Thought for the day: Who do I know that is struggling to cope, and what can I do to help them?

Nick Clarke (England, United Kingdom)

God can

Read 1 Peter 5:6–11

Cast all your anxiety on [God], because he cares for you.
1 Peter 5:7 (NIV)

When a women's retreat committee asked me to speak to them, God urged me to share my struggle with depression and how God brought people into my life in answer to my prayers. I did not want to be so vulnerable, but I trusted God's promise to give me the words and to take away my fear. It turned out that one young woman in particular needed to hear those words to know that she was not alone.

'I can't do it. I'm not as good as...' This type of thought often comes into my mind and makes me anxious. When God wanted me to share the truth of God's word with others, I responded in fear with, 'Me? I can't.' But God helped me overcome my fear.

God knows our needs, fears and even our lack of faith. We can go to God, hand over our cares and fears, and then let God guide us in what to do. I might not have the same abilities as my friends. 'I can't' is often still my first response. I am still learning how to give my fears, cares and anxieties to God. But I also know that just as God helped me speak about depression, God can help us all to do anything God asks of us.

Prayer: *Dear God, thank you for helping us to move past our fears. Help us to trust that you will equip us for the tasks you ask of us. Amen*

Thought for the day: God will guide me in whatever God has asked me to do.

Carol Harrison (Saskatchewan, Canada)

Our noisy world

Read 1 Kings 19:9–12

Be still, and know that I am God.
Psalm 46:10 (NIV)

From the time we wake up until the time we go to sleep, we're bombarded with noise. The alarm clock begins the cacophony, giving way to the morning news, the honking traffic and the blaring radio. Computers and phones chirp, beep and ring, constantly demanding our attention. Noise fills our ears and distracts our minds. 'I can't even hear myself think!' I often exclaim in frustration.

Sadly, the relentless noise doesn't just drown out my own thoughts; it also drowns out God's voice. Psalm 46:10 reminds us that if we want to experience a firm confidence that God is in control, we must quiet ourselves in spite of the world around us.

This might be as simple as refusing to turn on the TV, radio or computer on a given day until after we've read our Bible. Or it might mean praying on the way to work instead of listening to music or the radio. Taking a few moments for quiet reflection gives us the opportunity to listen for God's voice. Sometimes we can hear God shouting to get our attention; but more often, God speaks in the still, small voice of the Holy Spirit. And that's a sound we never want to miss.

Prayer: *Gracious God, help us to quiet ourselves amid the chaos around us so that we can hear your voice more clearly. Amen*

Thought for the day: In the quiet I can hear God's voice.

Lori Hatcher (South Carolina, USA)

Strength and peace

Read 2 Corinthians 12:2–10

[The Lord] said to me, 'My grace is sufficient for you, for my power is made perfect in weakness.' Therefore I will boast all the more gladly about my weaknesses, so that Christ's power may rest on me.
2 Corinthians 12:9 (NIV)

On Friday, 28 July 2017, my wife Lisa and I were shocked to hear my physician say, 'I think you have ALS.' I don't remember much after those words except for the moment I looked at Lisa's face and knew that our lives would change forever.

Further testing confirmed the diagnosis: amyotrophic lateral sclerosis, a fatal disease with no known cure. On average, patients survive only 2–5 years after diagnosis.

It took weeks for the reality of our unknown future to set in. However, there was one thing I was certain about: God was with me and would continue working through me! After sharing our news with family, close friends and our church, we received an outpouring of love through encouraging words, hugs, cards and visits.

In addition to receiving love, it has been my hope to share 'a peace that surpasses all understanding' with others (see Philippians 4:6–7). In line with Paul's words from today's reading, I try to give my weaknesses to God so that the Lord can use them. When friends and family tell me that they are praying for me and our family, I simply reply, 'Thank you' and add, 'God loves hearing your prayers!'

Prayer: *Heavenly Father, when we face trials that seem insurmountable, thank you for your love, mercy and grace, which provide us strength, hope and unexplained peace. Amen*

Thought for the day: God loves me and is present in every situation.

John Wesley 'Wes' Sexton (South Carolina, USA)

Trusting God

Read Exodus 17:1–7

Trust in the Lord with all your heart, and do not rely on your own insight. In all your ways acknowledge him, and he will make straight your paths.

Proverbs 3:5–6 (NRSV)

I had applied for a professional course at my university, but my name wasn't on the first provisional list of candidates chosen. When I saw this, I became anxious and blamed myself for foolishly not applying to other universities. Finally when I felt there was no way I would be accepted, I fasted and prayed. To my surprise, God heard my prayers on the very first day of my fast. I was selected in the second provisional list. I felt sheepish that I had been complaining for no reason. This was a miracle God was already about to perform!

The Israelites had a similar experience when God brought them to Rephidim. Instead of enjoying their new freedom, they complained about the lack of water. They started grumbling and complaining to Moses, rather than trusting that God who led them out of Egypt would sustain them. As a result of the complaining, Moses named the place 'testing' and 'complaining'. Maybe had they waited patiently and trusted God, they would still have enjoyed the miracle of water gushing from the rock at Horeb. But then the place could have been named 'trusting' and 'rejoicing' instead. In difficult situations, instead of putting God to the test, we can trust that God will care for us.

Prayer: *Help us, Lord, to trust you always. Amen*

Thought for the day: God sees my need and will always answer.

Carol Macwan (Gujarat, India)

A sense of urgency

Read Luke 15:8–10

Look to the Lord and his strength; seek his face always.
Psalm 105:4 (NIV)

Recently, my wife and I pulled into a restaurant parking lot and noticed that a vehicle backing out had something on the rear bumper. As we got closer, I could see it was a wallet. I jumped out, grabbed the wallet and went to the driver's door. The driver had a surprised look on her face, not quite sure what I was doing. But as soon as I held the wallet up, her eyes brightened with relief and thankfulness.

Today's scripture story shows how Jesus used our feeling of urgency when we've lost something to illustrate a point about salvation. Jesus, the good shepherd, searches intently for us; but sometimes I wonder how hard we search for Jesus. Do we have that same sense of urgency when it comes to following him and sharing the good news? Sometimes we may find that we've left Jesus on the rear bumper of our lives. We focus too much on our wants and needs and distance ourselves from Jesus – not realising we've left our most valuable possession behind.

We can always ask God to rekindle our urgency to seek and to share the love of Jesus. No matter how far we may have travelled, God is always there, ready to forgive and welcome us back.

Prayer: *Dear God, forgive us when we forget to prioritise our faith, and help us to pursue your wisdom as we journey day by day. Amen*

Thought for the day: Today I will search for Jesus as urgently as he seeks me.

Travis Teague (North Carolina, USA)

Waiting for God

Read Psalm 27:1–14

Wait for the Lord; be strong, and let your heart take courage; wait for the Lord!

Psalm 27:14 (NRSV)

My grandchildren live a continent away. When we are planning a visit, waiting to be reunited can seem to take an eternity for all of us. My daughter helps the children by marking off the number of sleeps left until they run down the airport ramp into my arms. Meanwhile, she calls their attention to the present by having them draw pictures, pack backpacks and buy gifts. They are learning to trust that the big day will come in good time.

In Psalm 27, David assented to the goodness of God while waiting for vindication. He sought God, wanting the Lord to teach him and remain close to him. David maintained a sense of living in the present while looking towards a hopeful future. Scripture teaches that waiting is a time of expectation, drawing near to God and gaining strength in the process.

The next time we find ourselves waiting with worry or impatience, we might ask: Where is God in this moment? What are the needs of those around me? What am I trying to control that is better left in God's hands?

Prayer: *Dear Lord, thank you for your patience with us when we wait with worry and frustration. Help us to draw strength and courage from you as we wait on your word. Amen*

Thought for the day: When we wait in faith, we will see the goodness of God.

Mary Wisner (Michigan, USA)

The narrow path

Read Luke 13:22–30

Jesus said, 'Make every effort to enter through the narrow door.'
Luke 13:24 (NIV)

Our village is crisscrossed by winding paths between the houses. Walls seven feet high protect the paths. I enjoy turning from the road through the narrow entrance on to the path because the wind drops, the sun shines a little warmer and the gardens look brighter. I am amazed by the huge flowers of the dinner-plate hibiscus, and I look for the shining black king skink moving away into the abundant ground cover. Out of the wind and extreme temperatures, the path is a sanctuary for me.

Similarly, we need the focus of a narrow door to fully appreciate the sanctuary of our life in Christ. The world offers us many competing treasures, but the only way we can be certain of lasting treasure is to follow Jesus through that narrow door where we join him on the path. This does not mean that we reject all the good things of the world. Instead, with Christ on the path with us, we are sufficiently focused so that we can appreciate their true value. Our relationships take on greater joy when we treat others with the love and care Christ shows us. Our perception of the world will be clearer when we remember the creator who brings it into being.

The narrow way is not primarily a restraint on our lives. Rather, it opens our lives to possibilities of living more fully with Christ.

Prayer: *Lead us, Lord, through the narrow door on to the narrow path where we may better recognise and appreciate your gifts to us. Amen*

Thought for the day: Following Christ through the narrow door allows me to live abundantly.

Ted Witham (Western Australia, Australia)

The person in front of you

Read John 8:1–11

The Lord is not slow in keeping his promise, as some understand slowness. Instead he is patient with you, not wanting anyone to perish, but everyone to come to repentance.
2 Peter 3:9 (NIV)

After moving to a suburb of a large metropolitan area, I felt discouraged and frightened by news stories of nearby criminal activity. It was hard to read about an armed robbery at a convenience store, a hit-and-run accident that injured a child or a group following a delivery truck to steal packages. My first response was to pray for the victims of these crimes. I could identify with the fear, grief and anger they must have felt. However, the more I let my prayers be guided by the news stories, the more concern I developed for the perpetrators. I asked myself, 'What circumstances would lead my neighbour to these kinds of actions?'

Second Peter 3 reminds me that God has been patient with my failings and deeply desires for all people to repent. I now feel called to pray not only for the victims but also for those who have committed crimes in my community.

I am also challenged to consider how I offer God's love and forgiveness to the people I encounter daily. My church encourages its members to 'love the person in front of you'. This means accepting people as they are instead of judging them. I try to remember these challenging words when I encounter people whose actions I do not understand. Then I ask Jesus to help me love them as he already does.

Prayer: *Forgiving Christ, help us to love and pray for people whose actions we cannot comprehend. Amen*

Thought for the day: Jesus loves every person in my community.

Beverly Marshall-Goodell (Georgia, USA)

Opportunities to obey

Read Luke 9:57–62

Jesus replied, 'No one who puts a hand to the plough and looks back is fit for service in the kingdom of God.'
Luke 9:62 (NIV)

Several years ago, I worked in sales. My sales partner was an energetic young man fresh out of college. After a few months, he started to become frustrated. 'I don't know how to make a dent in our market,' he would say.

One day after hearing his frustrations, I told him that since markets are made up of individual accounts we should try to focus on individual customers. We tried this approach and found success.

As Christians, we are also tempted to think in general terms. 'Give Jesus your life,' we rightly encourage one another. However, what does that mean? How do we actually do that?

Just like a market is made up of individual accounts, our lives are made up of individual moments. In these verses from Luke 9, Jesus challenges us to follow him, even amid the gritty, mundane reality of daily existence. Every moment, every circumstance is an opportunity for obedience.

Focusing on these daily opportunities allows us to break down our commitment to Christ into smaller, more manageable pieces. As we surrender each moment, we find our whole life conforming to God's plan.

Prayer: *Dear Lord, help us to see you in the ordinary moments of daily existence. Show us ways to submit our lives to you and to learn obedience. Amen*

Thought for the day: What small moments can I submit to Christ today?

Jason Koon (North Carolina, USA)

Grateful and generous

Read 2 Corinthians 9:10–15

You will be enriched in every way so that you can be generous on every occasion, and through us your generosity will result in thanksgiving to God.
2 Corinthians 9:11 (NIV)

My brother, Martín, lives in New York. In the apartment building where he lives, several cats come around every evening. My brother tells me that he always purchases food for them, spending about $10 daily. Knowing he has limited resources, his friends scold him and question why he bothers with the cats. My brother's response is: 'It is a way to express gratitude for God's immense goodness. I am almost 70 years old, and God has granted me a good life – without pain, filled with energy, and the ability to work and live without limitations. Caring for God's creatures is a small way to demonstrate my gratitude to God.'

As I reflected on his story, I realised that if we all expressed such gratitude to God, it would create in us a generous spirit; we would have a much more loving and caring world. I am grateful for my brother, for his example, and for his inspiration to follow the biblical teaching to 'be generous on every occasion'. May we all work at developing more grateful and generous hearts so that God's will may more fully be realised.

Prayer: *Generous God, thank you for your loving-kindness and the blessings we receive each day. Inspire us to be generous with everyone we can, in whatever ways we can. In the name of the one who gave his life for us. Amen*

Thought for the day: Today I will show gratitude to God by giving generously.

Yesenia Rosado (Dominican Republic)

Unexpected places

Read Psalm 145:17–21

The Lord is near to all who call on him, to all who call on him in truth. He fulfills the desires of those who fear him; he hears their cry and saves them.

Psalm 145:18–19 (NIV)

About a week after I returned from maternity leave, my job was unexpectedly eliminated. I was shocked, hurt and anxious about how my husband and I would make ends meet. We were *just* learning how to be parents of a new baby. How were we supposed to handle this?

I went grocery shopping the next day with a heavy heart, still wondering about the future. I saw a woman about my age who looked familiar. Asking her name, I realised that she was the nurse who helped me through the toughest part of my recent labour. She was a kind and patient caregiver, and I had wanted her to meet my daughter. But her shift ended before she had the chance. This had always made me a little sad. Three months later – in the middle of a grocery store – they finally had the chance to meet.

This was the sweetest moment that the Lord could have given me that day. I was scared, and God had felt far away. In that moment, I realised that God heard my prayers and listened closely. Our creator is always present and always lovingly cares for us, even when our situation feels troubled. Sometimes God speaks to us when we least expect it.

Prayer: *Dear Lord, help us to remember your goodness and faithfulness always. May we lean on you in times of distress, knowing that you hear our cries. Amen*

Thought for the day: God loves and cares for me always.

Amy Culwell (Alabama, USA)

An open mind

Read Isaiah 49:13–18

See, I have inscribed you on the palms of my hands.
Isaiah 49:16 (NRSV)

I knew no other students in my new sixth-grade class. I cried every day after school, and I felt alone, scared and empty. I begged my mum not to make me go and even asked her to homeschool me. I was afraid of being alone all day.

One day I was determined that I was not going to school. After my mum dropped me off at school, I ran away. I planned to go sit outside my house all day since no one would be home. As I walked home, my mum found me. She asked me what was wrong. When I told her everything, she told me that I really was not alone. She explained that God was with me, and had a plan for me. I decided to go to school with a mind open to God's plan, and I ended up making two friends who remain my closest friends to this day.

Even when we feel the most alone, God is with us. It is impossible for us to be alone if God is in our hearts. When we feel scared and alone, we can choose to focus on God's presence and plan for us. We can take refuge in Christ and let him be our guide.

Prayer: *Loving God, help us always to trust in you and be open to your plans for us. Remind us of your presence and guidance when we are lonely. Amen*

Thought for the day: God's presence in my life means I am never truly alone.

Jesse Cantu (Texas, USA)

First Sunday of Advent

Read John 8:12–20

Jesus spoke to them, saying, 'I am the light of the world. Whoever follows me will never walk in darkness but will have the light of life.'
John 8:12 (NRSV)

One time when our daughters were young, a big blizzard caused our power to go out. At first our daughters were afraid of the darkness. When my husband, Jim, and I lit our emergency candles, our girls enjoyed the bright, dancing flames. The light filled the darkness while we ate dinner and read bedtime stories.

There is something comforting about light when everything is dark and uncertain. Light gives us perspective, vision and hope. Jesus is the 'Light of the World' no matter what kind of darkness our world is experiencing.

Jesus promised that if we follow him we will never walk in darkness because his light shows us the way and gives abundant life. The light of Christ shines through us when we follow him faithfully. As we enter the season of Advent, we can let Christ's light shine through us and illuminate the darkness in our world.

Prayer: *O Christ, thank you for your light of life. Help us to remain focused on you in this season and always. Amen*

Thought for the day: I will let Christ's light shine through me today.

Laurel Balyeat Morrison (California, USA)

Worries into prayers

Read Philippians 4:4–9

Do not worry about anything, but in everything by prayer and supplication with thanksgiving let your requests be made known to God.

Philippians 4:6 (NRSV)

Worry is a natural, human response to challenging situations. Years ago I contracted life-threatening malaria and typhoid fever, and I worried I would die.

Then one day I felt God saying, 'Be still and know that I am God.' From that time on, I converted my worries and anxieties into prayers, and my faith in God grew. I studied more of God's word as I made my requests known to God. The apostle Paul told the Philippians not to be anxious about anything; rather, in whatever situation they found themselves, they should take all their petitions to God with thanksgiving.

God answers prayers. Dwelling on worries and doubts does no good; but when we bring our petitions to God with thanksgiving, praying with faith in our hearts, our prayers will be answered.

Prayer: *Lord Jesus, give us faith to release our worries and pray more. Help us always to be thankful for what you've done and what you will do. Amen*

Thought for the day: Today I will worry less and pray more.

Ubong E.A. Zeal (Akwa Ibom State, Nigeria)

A masterpiece

Read Psalm 8:1–9

We are God's handiwork, created in Christ Jesus to do good works, which God prepared in advance for us to do.
Ephesians 2:10 (NIV)

For the past few years, I have been studying how to paint with oils. At first, the technique was overwhelming. However, I am beginning to feel more comfortable with each new painting.

To begin any new work of art, I need an idea, brushes, oils and a blank canvas. Lately, I start by tracing a photograph and painting the background colours. Little by little, the artwork comes alive – and hopefully resembles the photo too.

It takes time and patience to create a finished product. This process helps me to understand the attention and care our Lord has taken to create each of us. God is the master artist. Scripture says that we are God's handiwork – not a duplicate but an individual masterpiece. We are fearfully and wonderfully made and remade by our faithful creator, who knows our innermost being. With God as our painter, we are called to rejoice at the beauty within ourselves and others.

Prayer: *Dear God, you are the master creator with an eye for detail. Help us to see each individual and ourselves with your eyes. Amen*

Thought for the day: Instead of judging myself and others, I will admire God's creations.

Denise L. Armstrong (Ohio, USA)

No need to fear

Read Deuteronomy 31:1–6

[The Lord] will never leave you nor forsake you.
Deuteronomy 31:6 (NIV)

I work in Kansas, which is a long way from my home in south-central Pennsylvania. After spending a wonderful week at home over Christmas with family and friends, I couldn't sleep the night before I was to return to Kansas. I felt anxious about leaving my family and being alone again in Kansas, as well as what the flight back would be like. As I lay awake in bed worrying, I decided to take comfort in God's word by reading that day's devotional in *The Upper Room*. The quoted scripture was from Deuteronomy: 'Be strong and courageous. Do not be afraid or terrified because of them, for the Lord your God goes with you; he will never leave you nor forsake you.' Those words spoke directly to my soul. I felt better knowing that no matter what the plane ride or future held for me, God would always be with me.

I know I will miss being with my wife and family when I am not physically with them. But I can take comfort in knowing that God is always with me, will never forsake me and will give me the strength I need to make it through until I can be home again.

Prayer: *Loving God, we thank you for your promise always to be with us. In our times of anxiety, help us to reach out to you and receive your peace. Amen*

Thought for the day: God will comfort me during any time of uncertainty.

Eric Gamber (Pennsylvania, USA)

Fully charged

Read Psalm 62:1–12

Yes, my soul, find rest in God; my hope comes from him.
Psalm 62:5 (NIV)

I was listening to some music on my portable CD player one day when suddenly the music sounded distorted and muffled. It was all jumbled, and it hardly sounded like music at all. I soon realised that the batteries were low, so I replaced them. Then the music was restored to its original clarity and beauty.

How like our walk with God! We can become so focused on how we are serving God that sometimes we do not pay attention to our spiritual health and fail to realise when our spiritual batteries run low. We think we can keep going and still hear God just as clearly. We forget that we need to spend regular time with God in prayer and worship to recharge our spirits so that we can better understand what God is saying to us. When we spend time with God, we can remain fully charged and have enough energy to complete the work God has for us to do.

Prayer: *Dear God, help us always to make time for you so that we can keep our spirits fully alive and ready to respond to your call. Amen*

Thought for the day: What will I do to recharge my spiritual batteries this week?

Carol Parker (England, United Kingdom)

Thick-skinned or too sensitive?

Read Ephesians 6:13–18

Be strong in the Lord and in his mighty power.
Ephesians 6:10 (NIV)

In a film I was watching, a small boy was seeking to control his huge but lovable elephant. When the boy called the elephant a 'pachyderm', I thought it was a term of abuse. Later, I learned that the word describes any large mammal with thick skin, such as an elephant, rhinoceros or hippopotamus; pachyderm literally means 'thick skin'.

Sometimes I wonder if I need to be more thick-skinned instead of being so sensitive and easily hurt. Yet if I were less sensitive, would I be aware of the pain and needs of others? God wants us to be tender-hearted, quick to apologise when we have trampled on the feelings of others and ready to share their burdens and feel their pain. But likewise God does not want us to fall into despair when we experience difficult times or receive harsh criticism.

The answer, as Paul wrote to the Ephesians, is not for us to 'toughen up', but to be strong in God and in the power of his might. God has given us his armour: the helmet of salvation, the breastplate of righteousness, the belt of truth, the shield of faith. Together with the word of God, this 'thick skin' will enable us to both withstand the enemy's attack and be ready to minister the peace of the gospel.

Prayer: *Lord, keep us tender-hearted, yet always strong and bold in you. Amen*

Thought for the day: How can I be more aware of the needs of others, especially those suffering from depression?

Pauline Lewis (Wales, United Kingdom)

Reconciling love

Read Genesis 33:1–10

Esau ran to meet him, and embraced him, and fell on his neck and kissed him, and they wept.
Genesis 33:4 (NRSV)

If ever anyone had reason to hold on to resentment, it was Esau. His younger brother Jacob stole his birthright by trickery and deceit (see Genesis 27:1–41). And yet, Esau forgave Jacob in an act of true brotherly love.

Jesus' parable of the prodigal son also speaks of forgiveness – a father's incredible affection for his son reunited a family (see Luke 15:11–32). In both stories, forgiveness and love combine in reconciliation.

One time at an airport, I saw the crowds greeting one another with embraces, kisses, smiles and a few tears. I wondered if any of these people were there to greet a prodigal or a Jacob. There are so many broken relationships in the world. In light of that pain, God's gift of reconciliation stands out starkly.

God models reconciling love through these Bible stories and also through Jesus Christ. As Paul explained, God reconciled us to God's self and each other through Jesus Christ (see 2 Corinthians 5:18).

Because of God's love and through the Holy Spirit, we all can be like Esau and the father of the prodigal son. We are able to say 'I'm sorry' or 'I forgive you', because we have first known the love of our creator through Jesus Christ.

Prayer: *Heavenly Father, teach us to love as you love. Bless us with a spirit of reconciliation so that we can apologise and forgive freely. Amen*

Thought for the day: What relationships in my life need reconciliation?

Anthony Lang (New South Wales, Australia)

Second Sunday of Advent

Read John 1:10–18

The Word became flesh and made his dwelling among us. We have seen his glory, the glory of the one and only Son, who came from the Father, full of grace and truth.
John 1:14 (NIV)

My third grandchild, Tinlie, arrived in the midst of my chemotherapy treatments for breast cancer. Discovering that an aggressive form of the disease was invading my body, I was devastated. Yet as I cradled my new granddaughter in my arms, I knew her birth had given me a renewed sense of purpose and much-needed hope. I was able to look beyond myself to God's gift of a new life.

How much more should the birth of our Saviour give us hope and a reason to share the good news with those around us? Scripture tells us that Jesus came to rescue us from our sin and to offer us eternity with him. What a reason for hope! From the wonder of Jesus' conception by the Holy Spirit, to his birth in a stable, to his sinless life on earth, his death and resurrection, Jesus' life of love gives us an abundance of hope!

Today, God's gift of Jesus continues to offer new life to all who feel they are without hope. God means for us to share this gift of love and hope with others.

Prayer: *Dear Father, thank you for the gift of Jesus and all that his birth means for us. Shine your light into the world so that everyone can experience the hope of new and eternal life through Jesus. Amen*

Thought for the day: The birth of Christ Jesus renews my hope.

Teresa Todt (Illinois, USA)

Godly interruptions

Read Matthew 25:31–46

Lord, when did we see you hungry or thirsty or a stranger or needing clothes or sick or in prison, and did not help you?
Matthew 25:44 (NIV)

Recently my wife, Gwen, and I were on holiday. Because there was no coffee available at our hotel, I took an early-morning stroll and found a fast-food restaurant nearby. The place was almost empty; but as I headed towards the counter, a man approached me and asked, 'Sir, would you buy me breakfast? I'm hungry but don't have any money.' I politely declined and continued towards the counter. 'Just another panhandler,' I thought.

My response had been a selfish reaction to an interruption, and I instantly regretted it. This man hadn't asked for money; he just wanted breakfast. If I had offered to pay for his meal, it could have been an opportunity to show God's love to someone. I quickly went back out to the street to look for him, but he was nowhere in sight.

As I write this, I still feel deep remorse. God has forgiven me, but nonetheless I grieve as I reflect on my reaction to what I feel was a godly interruption. God presents us with daily opportunities to grow and serve in the least likely places – and often at inconvenient times. When we stop focusing only on ourselves, we can be ready to respond when opportunities to show God's love arise.

Prayer: *Loving God, help us to be alert to each person you put in our path today. In Jesus' name we pray. Amen*

Thought for the day: Every day I will watch for Godly interruptions.

Tom Smith (Utah, USA)

Trust in the Lord

Read Luke 5:17–26

This is the day that the Lord has made; let us rejoice and be glad in it.
Psalm 118:24 (NRSV)

Our family recently lost my daughter-in-law Evelyn, and she will be deeply missed. Joy, the youngest of her eleven grandchildren, loved to run to her, wrap her arms around her legs, and tell her she'd never let her go. Much like the friends of the paralytic in our reading from Luke, my son Mike worked with hospital staff for weeks to fight the illness that enveloped Evelyn. In the end, her heart and kidneys couldn't go on.

We are not always ready to let go of our loved ones. However, if we follow God's word and trust God, the burden is lighter. Because I have been blessed with a very long life, I have had to endure many losses. I remember my mum, too, grieving that she was one of the last of her generation. But every day she would write in her journal, 'This is the day that the Lord has made. Let us rejoice and be glad in it.'

We are meant to cherish our days with gratitude for God's presence in our lives. Yet we understand that we are mortal and trust that our loved ones will keep us alive in their hearts. Joy may have to be reminded of her grandmother's big laugh, but we hope she will remember the love she and her grandmother shared.

Prayer: *Dear God, we rejoice in the gift of family. Even as we pray for miracles in the face of illness and pain, we hold on to the hope of your promise of eternal life. Amen*

Thought for the day: In the face of pain and loss, I will put my trust in the Lord.

Dolly Doss (Texas, USA)

No longer afraid

Read John 1:1–9
The people who sat in darkness have seen a great light, and for those who sat in the region and shadow of death light has dawned.
Matthew 4:16 (NRSV)

When I was young, I had a great fear of darkness. One night the electricity went off. Darkness quickly enveloped my room, and I felt something bad was closing in on me. I screamed until my mother rushed to my rescue. As soon as the light from her lantern shone into the room, the darkness disappeared!

Thinking about that night years later reminds me of how the whole world lay in darkness until God spoke the sun into being. I think also of how the coming of Jesus Christ as the true light dispelled the darkness in the world and illuminated the path for humankind (see John 1:9). Finally, thinking of that night reminds me of a cold manger in Bethlehem where the holy child was born. That night marks the point at which God shone a divine light into the world and dispelled the power of evil.

Remembering my experience with darkness as a child helps me understand Christmas better. Christmas is the time when God's light through Christ breaks the hold of sin in the world. I no longer celebrate Christmas blindly but with a deep understanding of what God did by sending Jesus as the light of the world.

Prayer: *God of light, fill our hearts with the joy of Christmas so that the light of the gospel can shine anew in the world. In Jesus' name. Amen*

Thought for the day: Christmas is the celebration of Jesus, the light of the world.

Olaiya Muyiwa Benralph (Federal Capital Territory, Nigeria)

Loving first

Read 1 John 4:19–21

We love because God first loved us.
1 John 4:19 (CEB)

Our hearts were broken. A few months earlier, we had lost our beloved dog. One day my husband and I felt it was time to visit the local animal shelter and look for a pet who might fill the hole in our hearts. And we found him! He was in a small cage with his head down and his tail between his legs. We thought, 'He needs us and we need him!' Now, only weeks after bringing him home, he runs to greet us, holds his tail up high, chases his ball nonstop and is the happiest dog.

If the love my husband and I gave to that little dog can completely change him in such a wonderful way, how much more can the love of God change all of us? 'We love because God first loved us' (1 John 4:19), and because God loved us first, we are able to do things that we couldn't possibly do otherwise. We can replace anger with forgiveness, we can replace prejudice with acceptance and we can work towards peace in our families, neighbourhoods and the world. We can love!

Prayer: *Dear God, help us not to wait for others to show love to us, but give us courage to love them first. Amen*

Thought for the day: Today I will look for opportunities to surprise others with acts of love.

Carola Spreacker (New Mexico, USA)

Focused on Jesus

Read Psalm 23:1–6

Let us run with perseverance the race marked out for us, fixing our eyes on Jesus, the pioneer and perfecter of faith.
Hebrews 12:1–2 (NIV)

When I was first learning to drive, I had the habit of looking directly at the ground in front of the car. Every rock, stick and pothole prompted me to react. I would steer first in one direction, then another, trying to avoid the slightest obstacle. My instructor finally asked me to pull over and offered some life-saving wisdom. He wanted me to focus my eyes on the horizon and to drive straight towards it. He explained that by lifting my gaze and locking in on a focal point in the distance, I would be able to steer more smoothly to my destination yet still be aware of my surroundings.

That advice not only improved my driving technique but also provided me a powerful spiritual insight. Our paths in life are frequently filled with hazards and tempting distractions. But it is important for us to keep our sight trained on the horizon that is Jesus, who will help us navigate through anything we face. Jesus is master of both the calm and the storm and can guide us safely.

The spiritual disciplines of praying, meditating on scripture and participating in Christian fellowship can help us increase our focus on Jesus and lead us to our fullest lives.

Prayer: *Dear God, help us keep our eyes fixed on your ways. Guide our paths daily as we walk both with you and towards you. Amen*

Thought for the day: Today I will focus my thoughts on Jesus.

James Stewart (Illinois, USA)

Welcoming with open arms

Read Joshua 2:8–15, 21

God does not have favourites.
Romans 2:11 (CEB)

'She's not like us,' the woman said as we cleaned the church kitchen. Smiling, I turned to her and said, 'And isn't that great?' Unmoved, she walked away without replying.

When we truly open the doors of our churches and our hearts, we need to be ready for people who are 'not like us'. If we greet them with acceptance, not just tolerance, we open ourselves to a variety of experiences. New people, different people, can lead to diversity in music, in dress and maybe even in the menu for church luncheons.

As my sister in Christ expressed her discomfort with someone who wasn't like her, I wonder if that was how the women of Israel discussed Rahab when she joined them. Did they consider her unworthy of divine purpose because her life was so very different from theirs? Did they feel more worthy than she to be used for God's plan?

The timeless beauty communicated in Rahab's story is that the outsider is loved and welcomed into the loving heart of God. As the people of God, Christians are called to carry out this hospitality on earth.

Today, let's look at each person we pass with open and loving eyes. Let's step beyond tolerance into acceptance and learn to love others for their place in God's plan.

Prayer: *Dear God, give us open hearts, minds and eyes to see how beautiful our differences can be. Help us to trust your creativity. Amen*

Thought for the day: Who is God inviting me to welcome into my community?

Kimberly Rice Smith (North Carolina, USA)

Third Sunday of Advent

Read Matthew 1:18–23

'Look, the virgin shall conceive and bear a son, and they shall name him Emmanuel,' which means, 'God is with us.'
Matthew 1:23 (NRSV)

Just 14 days before Christmas, our father died. Christmas for our family will never be the same again. While everyone is celebrating, having reunions and exchanging gifts, I don't know how Christmas is going to be joyful for me and my family. As I gaze at the twinkling lights on our Christmas tree, my eyes well up with tears. Papa's passing was a shock to us. No words can describe our sadness. My memories of Papa are clear in my mind, but sometimes memories aren't enough to soothe the pain. When my friends and colleagues ask me how I am doing, I can't really say I'm okay; all I can say is that I'm still holding firmly to God.

Even as I grieve, I will still celebrate Christmas. After all, the name Emmanuel means 'God is with us'. Jesus has felt the pain that we feel; I believe that's why his presence gives me peace during my grieving. And while grieving lasts a long time, I know I'm not alone because God holds on to me even tighter. Though I lost my loving earthly father, my heavenly Father will carry me – this Christmas and each day of my life.

Prayer: *Lord Jesus, thank you for the peace that you give us and the assurance that you are with us in our painful moments. Comfort all who grieve during this Christmas season. Amen*

Thought for the day: When we are most in need, God is closer than ever.

Karen Tarine (National Capital Region, Philippines)

Follow the leader

Read 1 Corinthians 10:31–11:1

Paul wrote, 'Follow my example, as I follow the example of Christ.'
1 Corinthians 11:1 (NIV)

'Follow the Leader' was a favourite childhood game which I played with my sister and cousin. One of us would serve as the leader, while the other two were to mimic the leader's movements. It could be a simple act like touching our toes, or a more challenging one such as throwing a ball through a hoop. The one who could not duplicate the leader's actions would be out. Eventually, we were each eliminated and a new person would serve as leader for the next round.

Following and leading are what servants of Christ are called to do. The apostle Paul sought to faithfully follow Christ. In doing so, he served as an example for others to follow. Jesus Christ calls each one of us to follow him as well. Like the apostle Paul, our aim is not only to follow our Lord faithfully but to lead others to follow him too. As we move through our daily routine at work, at school, or at home, our actions are being viewed and evaluated by others. By living a life that models the life of Christ, we are directing others to an abundant life – a life that has eternal meaning and purpose. So as we 'Follow the Leader' we can lead others to follow in the way of discipleship.

Prayer: *Heavenly Father, help us to be models of faithful discipleship for all to see. In the name of the Christ whom we follow. Amen*

Thought for the day: How am I leading others to Christ?

Wayne Greenawalt (Illinois, USA)

God's will?

Read Romans 8:35–39

God is our refuge and strength, a help always near in times of great trouble.
Psalm 46:1 (CEB)

On 14 December 2012, a man forced his way into Sandy Hook School in Connecticut, shooting and killing 20 year-one children and six adults. I survived that massacre, but I saw and heard things that day that no one should ever have to experience.

At church, friends would ask me, 'How can I help?' I would answer, 'Please pray for me because I can't.' I was angry with God, wondering, 'How could it be God's will for these children to be killed? Why was I spared at age 60?' It made no sense. My faith was tested, and I struggled greatly.

A year later, my husband and I participated in a book study at church. The discussion focused on understanding God's will and trusting God's ways. The study brought me great clarity, because it helped me to realise that it *wasn't* God's will for 26 people to die. Rather, our loving God has given us all free will, and sin often prevails. I no longer blamed God. I understood that pure evil entered the school that day.

I couldn't have come this far in my trauma journey without my family, my friends and my faith in our loving God. Since that horrific day, I have learned how resilient God has made us. I have also learned never to take life for granted.

Prayer: *Dear God, help us to be kinder, gentler, more connected to one another. Surround us with your love. Amen*

Thought for the day: Even in my darkest hour, God will never abandon me.

Becky Virgalla (Connecticut, USA)

'Trapped' in the airport

Read Romans 12:9–16

Seek the welfare of the city where I have sent you.
Jeremiah 29:7 (NRSV)

'We're calling because we need your prayers, Pastor. We are trapped between flights in Chicago because of the snowstorm.' Our pastor asked, 'Are you inside where it is dry and climate controlled?' 'Yes,' I replied. 'Do you have access to water and food?' Again, I said, 'Yes.' Then he asked, 'Are you sick?' I answered, 'No.' He said to me, 'Then you aren't really trapped, are you? I'll pray for you to be of service to the Lord where you are.' We prayed together, and my attitude changed almost immediately.

I bought children's books at an airport store and offered them to families with children. My wife struck up a conversation with an older man wearing a Korean War veteran's hat. Later we offered to wait in the food line for others. It became easy for us to approach others, knowing we were all in the same situation. Additionally, several worried-looking, stranded passengers accepted our offer to pray with them.

The 16 hours in the terminal went rather quickly when we made ourselves available to others. We were not trapped. We were in the right place at the right time to reflect the love of God.

Prayer: *Dear Lord, when we feel trapped, show us how to be a witness to your loving presence. Amen*

Thought for the day: In any stressful circumstance, I can look for ways to serve God.

Leland P. Gamson (Indiana, USA)

The work of the Spirit

Read John 14:15–26

'The Advocate, the Holy Spirit, whom the Father will send in my name, will teach you all things and will remind you of everything I have said to you.'
John 14:26 (NIV)

When I enrolled in the Bible academy, I had the feeling that along the way I would forget what I had been taught. I had this same feeling when I attended small study groups or listened to sermons that had special meaning for me. I prayed that God would allow me to treasure and remember what I had learned.

Later on I took part in another study group based on the characteristics of a Christian disciple. That study helped me to understand that it is not necessary to overburden our minds with copious information we have heard or studied. It is not solely by our own efforts that God's word takes root and bears fruit in our lives but through the work of the Holy Spirit.

In today's scripture reading, we learn that the Holy Spirit is with each of us and will remind us of what we need to know. How gratifying it is to know that we are not alone! Through the work of the Holy Spirit we can count on God's wisdom and love to guide us every day.

Prayer: *We are grateful, God, for the Holy Spirit, who inspires us to open our minds, our eyes, and our understanding to follow where you lead. Amen*

Thought for the day: The Holy Spirit helps me bear the fruit of God's word.

Mayerling Moreno Valdiris (Miranda, Venezuela)

116   **PRAYER FOCUS:** BIBLE STUDY GROUPS

Prayers never die

Read Revelation 5:1–8

When [the Lamb] had taken the scroll, the four living creatures and the twenty-four elders fell before the Lamb, each holding a harp and golden bowls full of incense, which are the prayers of the saints.
Revelation 5:8 (NRSV)

Years after Jesus' death, John of Patmos received an incredible vision. He saw the heavenly throne room, the lamb of God, the great communion of saints, and something that I tend to overlook: there, in the throne room of God, in the hands of the elders, were golden bowls full of prayers. Rising up like incense before the throne of God are the prayers of God's people.

Every petition, every longing and deep desire, every intercession, every cry, every prayer ever offered is floating like incense before God's throne. Whenever I feel discouraged, as though something is amiss in my life, I remember this image from Revelation and imagine my prayer in the throne room of God. God deeply and intimately cares for us and wants us to live full and abundant lives. And even though we may not always see God working, we can trust that our prayers rise before God and that they will be answered in God's way and God's timing – for our good and God's glory.

Prayer: *Dear Father, thank you for the eternal life that you offer us through your Son, Jesus. Help us to keep an eternal perspective as we walk through each day. Amen*

Thought for the day: Today, I will confidently trust God for all that I need.

Stephen Hopkins (Tennessee, USA)

Surrendering worry

Read 2 Corinthians 4:16–18

I have told you these things, so that in me you may have peace. In this world you will have trouble. But take heart! I have overcome the world.
John 16:33 (NIV)

In Melbourne, Australia, you can experience four seasons in one day. And everyone has an opinion about which one is the best. Sometimes I feel like my life is like the weather. There are good seasons and bad seasons, good days and bad days. On some bad days, all I can do is think about the terrible things that could happen or how my life will never change.

God, however, invites me to think and live differently. Jesus tells us in Matthew 6:34 that we are not designed to know what the future holds. All we can do is deal with today's problems and trust God with tomorrow.

If we worry about bad times to come, we can miss out on the good in our lives. Worrying is as futile as staying inside on a beautiful day because the forecast may include thunderstorms. No! Good times are like vitamin D for the soul and sustain us through the tough times.

Jesus said we will have troubles, but he also said in the same breath to take heart, to be confident and of good cheer, undaunted and filled with joy because he has overcome it all.

Prayer: *Dear Lord, give us the wisdom to see what actions we can take today to find and offer joy as we surrender our future to you. Amen*

Thought for the day: I will take time to name my pain and joy and surrender it all to God.

Shelley Marolla (Victoria, Australia)

Fourth Sunday of Advent

Read Matthew 5:14–16

[God's] word is a lamp for my feet, a light on my path.
Psalm 119:105 (NIV)

My wife and I, along with the help of our children and grandchildren, have the tradition of picking out a live Christmas tree each year. My wife and grandkids are in charge of decorating the tree, and they do an awesome job. But before the first ornament is hung, it's my job to string the lights.

Last Christmas the corner where we placed the tree was rather dark and gloomy. As I added each strand of lights, the tree slowly began to brighten. By the time I added the star at the top, the entire tree was illuminated.

When I saw how each light lit up its section of the tree, it reminded me of how as followers of Christ we are called to shine brightly in our own corner of the world. God does not call any single person to 'light' the whole world – just to shine for those we come into contact with each day. We can treat others with compassion instead of harshness; we can compliment instead of complain. When we do this, others will see Jesus in us, and God's light and love will shine in every corner of the earth.

Prayer: *Heavenly Father, help us to brighten someone's day with your love through an encouraging word, an act of kindness or simply a smile. Amen*

Thought for the day: I can be God's light for someone whose world seems dark.

Patrick Baumer (Indiana, USA)

Wonderfully made

Read Psalm 139:7–18

I praise you because I am fearfully and wonderfully made.
Psalm 139:14 (NIV)

I always had problems with my appearance. I compared myself to other girls and thought things like, 'Wow, if I had her hair, or her eyes, or her body…' This led to depression and suicidal thoughts. In summer 2018 I decided I didn't want to continue with this sadness anymore, and I grabbed some pills. I stood at the end of my bed completely heartbroken. That night a war was going on in my head. Thoughts swirled in my mind: 'Do it. You are worthless. No one is going to miss you.' But I also heard, 'Your family loves you. It isn't your time; I brought you into this world for a purpose. Hang in there, it will get better.' I knew God was with me as I struggled with these thoughts.

Psalm 139 reminds me that I am uniquely made by a God who loves us all unconditionally and sees us with loving eyes. Song of Songs 4:7 says, 'You are altogether beautiful, my darling; there is no flaw in you.' Each of us is beautiful and loved, and we are perfect in God's eyes. When we stop comparing ourselves to others, we can value ourselves for who we are. We are the children of God, and God loves us unconditionally despite our differences. We are fearfully and wonderfully made.

Prayer: *Dear God, teach us to value and love ourselves. Help us to stop comparing ourselves to others and instead to walk with confidence as the unique people you made us to be. Amen*

Thought for the day: I am God's masterpiece.

Perla Yaneth (Texas, USA)

Rooted in love

Read Ephesians 3:14–21

I pray that you, being rooted and established in love, may have power… to grasp how wide and long and high and deep is the love of Christ.

Ephesians 3:17–19 (NIV)

I have moved to a different part of the country a total of eleven times. As I write this I am about to move again to be near one of my sons and his family some distance away from my present home. I am in my eighties and have lived here almost 17 years, which is the longest time I've spent in the same house and town. Every move means leaving behind good friends and sometimes family members, then adjusting and settling in to a new home, new church, new surroundings, new job or stage of retirement, and making new friends.

However, the Lord has always given me a relevant text to confirm God's guidance and strength for each of my moves. This time it was the reassurance the Lord gave to Moses in Exodus 33:14: 'My Presence will go with you, and I will give you rest.'

What matters most is how we are rooted before and after a move. Paul's prayer for the Christians in Ephesus underlines that being firmly rooted in faith in Christ is the surest way to be resilient, to grow and to produce fruit where we have been planted. If we are rooted in the love of Christ, we have nothing to fear because we know that God will be with us.

Prayer: *Thank you, Lord, that we can step into the future confidently because we know you are with us. Amen*

Thought for the day: When I am rooted in Christ's love, I can feel at home anywhere.

Hazel V. Thompson (England, United Kingdom)

Different kind of miracle

Read Isaiah 41:1–10

Do not fear, for I am with you; do not be dismayed, for I am your God. I will strengthen you and help you; I will uphold you with my righteous right hand.

Isaiah 41:10 (NIV)

Years ago a friend of mine was in a car accident. Doctors found she had permanent damage to her spine and was paralyzed from the rib cage down. When I went to see her, she assured me that her condition was not permanent because God would not leave her like this and would perform a miracle.

As time went on, she did her therapy and coped with her circumstances – waiting for her miracle. Her faith never faltered even as her house was remodelled to accommodate her needs. She had a small store set up on her porch where she sold crafts and other personal items. One day I went to visit her at her 'store'. As I was browsing, I saw her stylish high heels lined up in a row – for sale. I began to cry; I knew she had accepted her fate.

Though the miracle she had hoped and prayed for hadn't come, I wondered whether another miracle of acceptance and faith had occurred. Her faith in God remained strong even in these circumstances. No matter what happens, God does not leave us alone. Sometimes that's the miracle.

Prayer: *Heavenly Father, thank you for your presence in our lives and for the knowledge that we are never alone. Thank you for the miracles you perform in our lives and for the assurance of your love and acceptance. In Jesus' name. Amen*

Thought for the day: Today I will look for God's unexpected miracles.

Grace Epperson (Michigan, USA)

Making space

Read Ephesians 4:25–32

Be kind to one another, tenderhearted, forgiving one another, as God in Christ has forgiven you.
Ephesians 4:32 (NRSV)

Our kitchen sink was not draining. We tried several clog removers, but nothing seemed to work. With no other option, I got out my tools and took apart the pipes. It was simultaneously amazing and disgusting. After I physically pulled smelly debris from the blocked pipes, water once again flowed freely.

Forgiveness is a lot like that process of breaking down and cleaning those pipes. Bitterness, anger and resentment clog up our lives. Often, we just want to ignore the problem or find an easy fix. While those may seem to work for a bit, eventually the pain and rancour build up once again.

True forgiveness takes effort. It requires us to take out our tools and remove the debris that builds up in our hearts and makes it difficult to have compassion for others. We can do this only because God has forgiven us first. Once we offer that grace to others and release them completely from their debt, our own lives can open back up.

Forgiveness makes space in our lives for the good things – God's grace, love and kindness – to flow freely. When that happens, it is better for us and better for everyone around us.

Prayer: *Dear God, give us the desire and power to forgive others. Clear our lives of resentment and anger so we can forgive and make space for love. Amen*

Thought for the day: Forgiving is hard, but God's grace makes it possible.

Bob LaForge (New Jersey, USA)

Christmas Eve

Read Luke 1:26–37

Faith is confidence in what we hope for and assurance about what we do not see.
Hebrews 11:1 (NIV)

I live in a two-season tropical country where churches have large windows and vents to keep us cool in the summer. During one Christmas service, wind and rain came into the church during the candle-lighting procession, making it hard for the congregation to keep the candles burning. A few times I had to ask the person sitting next to me to relight my candle.

The birth of Jesus is a symbol of hope following the long wait for the Saviour as our peacemaker. For me, the candlelight procession on that Christmas Eve symbolises my efforts to keep my hope and faith alive in a world full of uncertainty and chaos.

It is hard to hold on to faith and hope when prayers seem unanswered and reality does not match our expectations. In times like this, through reading the Bible and asking our fellow Christians to pray for our faith to be strengthened, we can keep the flame of hope alive.

Prayer: *God Almighty, thank you for giving us Jesus Christ. Help us to keep peace and hope alive in our hearts. We pray as Jesus taught us, 'Our Father which art in heaven, Hallowed be thy name. Thy kingdom come. Thy will be done, as in heaven, so in earth. Give us day by day our daily bread. And forgive us our sins; for we also forgive every one that is indebted to us. And lead us not into temptation; but deliver us from evil.'* Amen*

Thought for the day: Amid the uncertainty in the world I can look to scripture to keep my faith strong.

Juita Kartini (Jakarta, Indonesia)

Christmas Day

Read Luke 2:4–7

Each of you should give what you have decided in your heart to give, not reluctantly or under compulsion, for God loves a cheerful giver.
2 Corinthians 9:7 (NIV)

I sometimes feel sorry for the poor Bethlehem innkeeper in all our modern Christmas stories and plays. He is usually depicted as a mean man who somehow should have been able to manufacture a room for Joseph and the pregnant Mary. Instead, he sent them out into the cruel dark night. But the innkeeper had no space. He may have already had people sleeping in the halls and on the kitchen floor because of the huge crowds that had come for the census.

So, perhaps we can see the innkeeper in a different light. He offered what he had. He could have just told them to go away, but he figured out what he had left that might help and let them use his barn. I'm sure Mary and Joseph were very glad to get out of the elements and have a sheltered birthing place.

When a ministry needs a large amount of money for a mission or a friend needs many hands to help, we can't give them everything they need or do all the work by ourselves. But we can pray, and, as the innkeeper did, give what we have. When we give our best in God's name, it is good for us to remember what God gave – his Son.

Prayer: *Loving God, you have given us our talents and our lives; help us to use them for your purposes today. In Jesus' name. Amen*

Thought for the day: Regardless of the circumstance, I can always do my part to serve God.

Ken Claar (Idaho, USA)

Never alone

Read Proverbs 23:22–25

Each of you must respect your mother and father, and you must observe my Sabbaths. I am the Lord your God.
Leviticus 19:3 (NIV)

My dad passed away a few years ago. I often remember him, particularly when I am in an emotional downturn. I miss his support. I remember his goodness. He would always cook for us and leave us the best food. He carried heavy items for us. He was a fighter, undergoing many big surgeries and invasive medical checkups. He would do all of this with courage and independence.

Yet, he was not perfect. We often had arguments because he was stubborn and didn't listen to others. He struggled to understand what my sister and I felt and thought. He rarely cared about what we studied at school or how we spent our days at work.

My father had good and bad characteristics. However, in our family, my father's biggest legacy was leading us to God. He can no longer cook for us. Nor can he walk next to us and carry our shopping bags. But because of him, we met God and we believe in the Lord.

So, I am not an orphan. I am not alone. I know both God and my father cheer my family on to finish our race.

Prayer: *Dear God, thank you for parents and all their successes and failures. Thank you for being our perfect heavenly parent. Amen*

Thought for the day: God is my perfect heavenly parent.

Flo Au (Hong Kong, China)

Sacrificial love

Read John 15:12–14

No one has greater love than to give up one's life for one's friends.
John 15:13 (CEB)

The Christmas pantomime is a traditional feature of this time of year. I recall going to the theatre around Christmas time when I was six years old to see *Peter Pan*. I became completely swept up in the drama. There was a terrifying ticking crocodile, pirates and, of course, Peter Pan himself, who could fly. Tinkerbell, a fairy, was represented on the stage by a flickering light that moved around to the sound of a tinkling bell. I was spellbound!

At the climax of the show, Tinkerbell, in an act of love for Peter, deliberately drinks poison intended to kill him. As she is dying, her light begins to fade and become motionless. The audience has to bring her back to life by calling out, in typical pantomime fashion, 'I do believe in fairies.' Imagine my relief at her recovery.

This story is a reminder to me of the real story of Christmas. Although Christmas is a time when we celebrate Jesus' birth, rather than his death, Tinkerbell's act of sacrificial love, and subsequent coming back to life, is a reminder of why the baby Jesus came – to be our Saviour. When Jesus grew to adulthood, he gave his life in a sacrificial act of love that we might be forgiven. Though sinless, he died a painful, criminal's death on a cross that we might have eternal life.

And just as God raised Jesus from the dead, God promises to raise us also, if we are, as it were, willing to cry out, 'I do believe in Jesus!'

Prayer: *Thank you, Lord Jesus, that you died for each of us. Thank you that you promise us eternal life if we trust and obey you. Amen*

Thought for the day: Jesus gave his life for me!

Faith Ford (England, United Kingdom)

Resting in God's will

Read Matthew 11:28–30

Come unto me, all ye that labour and are heavy laden, and I will give you rest.

Matthew 11:28 (KJV)

I had retired from my job of over 20 years, and my children were all grown with families of their own. My once-hectic schedule of being a working mum seemed to come to a screeching halt. I should have been relishing this newfound slower pace. After all, wasn't this what I had looked forward to during those busy, exhausting years? Yet I found myself slightly depressed and feeling a sense of failure. I felt guilty that I was not accomplishing more in my life. I felt restless and like a fish out of water.

Finally, I did something I wish I had done earlier: I prayed about these feelings. The Lord began to remind me gently of things I was accomplishing. God also reminded me that I didn't need to keep up the former breakneck speed of my schedule. This was a different season of my life, and the pace could be slower.

I felt God's encouragement all through my spirit. I realised that those whispers of guilt and discouragement were not what God wanted for me. I began to view my schedule through a different lens. I felt hope, relief and a new energy. I was where I should be and was able to rest in that comforting truth.

Prayer: *Thank you, Father God, for guiding our lives. Help us to trust in your perfect will. Amen*

Thought for the day: God has a special purpose for every season in our lives.

Belle Todd (Texas, USA)

Change the world

Read Luke 6:37–49

Why do you call me 'Lord, Lord,' and do not do what I tell you?
Luke 6:46 (NRSV)

My friend Adam and I were camping, celebrating my decision to follow Christ. As I sat by the campfire, wrestling with the responsibility of my new faith, I felt a firm encouraging hand on my shoulder. I knew it was Jesus – Emmanuel, God with us.

I once would not have appreciated God's presence with me. When I was young, there was a Christian television ad which claimed that 'God might not change your circumstances, but he certainly changes you.' Back then I didn't want to be changed; I just wanted God to fix things with miracles like those in the Bible.

Only after my fireside encounter with Christ, as I read the whole Bible for myself, did I see beyond the miracles. Jesus expected his followers to live out his teachings by doing for others and choosing God over power. I discovered that discipleship means being transformed so that we can help change the world rather than sitting back and waiting for God to change it for us.

Being a Christian means not just saying 'Lord, Lord' but doing what Jesus said. Following Christ's teachings is scary sometimes, uncomfortable at others. It can cost us money, jobs, friends, family, even our lives. But God promises to be with us as we walk the way of Christ, being changed ourselves so that we can change the world together.

Prayer: *Dear God, as we walk with you, help us continue to change to become more like Christ so that with you we can change the world. Amen*

Thought for the day: With Christ's help, I can change the world.

Jason John (New South Wales, Australia)

Overcoming sadness

Read Psalm 30:1–12

You turned my wailing into dancing; you removed my sackcloth and clothed me with joy.

Psalm 30:11 (NIV)

Every once in a while I'm overwhelmed by fears that my cancer will return. The fear often catches me off guard and leads me to despair. I don't relish the sad days, but I know it's okay to have them. On the hard days, however, I know that God still loves me. As I endure the melancholy and tears, I know the pain will eventually pass.

Recently, on the evening of a sad day, a group of my son's friends came for dinner. They come every week and fill my house with laughter while they eat my mediocre cooking. My sadness almost caused me to cancel the gathering, but something happened as they all happily crammed around our dining table. My sadness lifted and was replaced with joy. Those boys will likely never know it, but God used their happiness to bring me peace.

Much in life can bring deep sadness. But God is good and a giver of good things. Life itself is a gift. My sons are a gift. Their friends are a gift. My time on this earth is a gift – every sad second and every joy-filled moment.

Prayer: *Dear God, thank you that you are always with us – even in our deep sadness. Thank you for the beautiful ways that you show up to bring us joy. Amen*

Thought for the day: Sadness will come, but God's gift of joy will follow.

Kim Harms (Iowa, USA)

Still on the boat

Read Mark 4:35–41

When you pass through the waters, I will be with you; and when you pass through the rivers, they will not sweep over you.
Isaiah 43:2 (NIV)

I was preparing for an entrance exam. I had failed the exam the previous year, and I was very stressed. I was not sure what to do. My mum called me one day and realised I was scared. She reminded me of the story in our reading today. She said, 'Jenny, Jesus may have appeared to be sleeping, but he was still on the boat!' With Jesus on the boat with his disciples, there was no chance that they would have drowned! That reminded me that whatever I may be facing, I am never alone. Christ is with me and will see me through.

I have often felt unsure of what to do. Sometimes it feels like Jesus is sleeping when I am in a storm. But I have learned that he is still on the boat with me even if he is silent in the moment. It may seem like I am going to drown, but Jesus is with me. Since coming to this realisation, I have failed more exams and passed others; I have taken a few risks and second-guessed myself a million times. But through it all I have never forgotten that Jesus is still on the boat with me.

Prayer: *Dear Lord, sometimes our storms are so frightening that we forget you are with us. Help us to trust you to take us safely to the other shore. In Jesus' name we pray. Amen*

Thought for the day: Rather than focusing on the storm, I will focus on Jesus, who is always with me.

Jennifer Prince Kingsley (Alabama, USA)

Small group questions

Wednesday 1 September

1 When you are faced with an obstacle, do you find it easy to remain positive or do you lose hope and feel discouraged? Where do you find encouragement during trying times?

2 Describe a recent situation when God provided for you. How did you praise and thank God for that provision?

3 Is it easy for you to praise God before you see the outcome of a situation? Why or why not? How does the Israelites' example inspire you to praise God before your breakthroughs?

4 How do you respond to God when you do not receive the outcome you prayed for? How do you trust God's will when the breakthrough you are hoping for doesn't come?

5 Who in the Bible reminds you of the importance of trusting God through adversity? How did God provide for this person? How does their story encourage you?

Wednesday 8 September

1 When has someone treated you in a way that felt disrespectful? Did you share your feelings with this person or keep them to yourself? Is there ever a time when someone doesn't deserve respect? Explain.

2 What scripture passages remind you of the importance of treating everyone with love and respect? Which of these scripture passages challenge you the most?

3 Today's writer used her feelings of shame as encouragement to grow spiritually. How does our relationship with God enable us to do this?

4 What do you think God sees when God looks at you? What does God see when God looks at others? How does it affect our relationships with other people when we try to see them as God does?

5 How does your faith community help you to love those whom you struggle to love? What ministries help your faith community to show love to others?

Wednesday 15 September

1 What daily rituals help you to live out your faith? How does your daily routine strengthen your faith?

2 Recall an important lesson that you learnt as a child. How might your life have turned out differently had you not learnt this lesson?

3 Where do you most clearly see God's grace in your life? Where do you see it in the lives of your loved ones?

4 When have you been surprised by something God has done in your life? In what ways did this change how you think about grace?

5 Describe how your loved ones and your faith community help you to deepen your relationship with God. How do those around you serve as examples of God's love and grace? In what ways does spending time with God and others fortify you to face life's storms?

Wednesday 22 September

1 Have you ever attended a worship service in a denomination other than your own? If so, what was your experience? What did you learn? In what ways can we benefit from worshipping God in a new, unfamiliar style?

2 What style of worship do you prefer? What do you like best about that style? What challenges does worshipping God in a new way pose? What opportunities might it create?

3 Why do you think God created so much diversity among people? In what ways is this a blessing? In what ways is it a challenge? Name something you have learnt from someone who is different from you.

4 Name some scripture passages that encourage us to live and worship in harmony with other Christians. How can we apply these passages to our relationships?

5   How does your faith community connect with Christians of different denominations or worship styles? In what ways could this strengthen Christian unity?

Wednesday 29 September

1   Describe a time when you were shown hospitality. How did it make you feel? What did it teach you about hospitality?

2   Is your way of showing hospitality more like Mary or Martha? Does it depend on the situation? Name some of the pros and cons of both approaches.

3   Do you find it easy or difficult to listen to others? What spiritual practices help you to be a better listener?

4   Today's writer says that listening is a spiritual gift and skill. What other spiritual gifts and skills are important when showing others God's love?

5   How well does your church community listen to those to whom it offers assistance? How might it listen better? What are the benefits of good listening?

Wednesday 6 October

1   What helps you the most when you are worried or afraid? What do you pray at those times?

2   Describe a time when you saw God in an ordinary moment. How did this experience bless you? How do you ensure that you are paying attention to the small ways that God is at work in your life?

3   Where do you notice God's peace and healing most clearly? What keeps you connected to God during stressful circumstances?

4   When is it easy to overlook the ordinary blessings you receive each day? How can you remind yourself to look for the blessings in ordinary moments as well as extraordinary ones? How do you thank and praise God in the ordinary?

5 How can you show God's love and peace to others in ordinary ways this week? How might you make the most of the ordinary moments God gives you?

Wednesday 13 October

1 Describe a time when you were well equipped for a task. Describe a time when you were ill-equipped for a task. How did the outcomes differ? What did you learn from each?

2 What does it look like for you to be prepared for your life's journey? What prayers and spiritual practices help to equip you?

3 Do you enjoy reading the Bible? What do you do when you read a part of the Bible that is confusing or hard to understand? If you could ask God one question about something you've read in the Bible, what would it be?

4 Who in scripture was well equipped? What do you most admire about those persons? How can you be more like them in your daily life?

5 Today's writer says that meditating on God's word can equip us for our life's journey. What are some of the positive outcomes that meditating on God's word can have in our lives?

Wednesday 20 October

1 How has your church been affected by the Covid-19 pandemic? What new ministries have come about as a result?

2 When have you felt dismayed at a situation only to find that good things came out of it? What does that teach you about yourself, about life and about God?

3 How are you intentional about connecting with God and with others? How did you begin these practices? How have your relationships changed as a result?

4 What are some advantages of thinking about church as a community rather than a place? How does your church extend its reach beyond its building?

5 When do you find it most difficult to connect to God or to those around you? How do you respond when you feel isolated? What brings you back into connection?

Wednesday 27 October

1 Talk about a time when what was on the outside of a place, of another person or of yourself did not match what was on the inside. Why are outward appearances sometimes different from what's on the inside? When is this okay? When is it not?

2 Recall a time when what you felt on the inside was not the same as what others saw on the outside. What helped you bring the two into closer alignment?

3 Do you find it comforting or unsettling to know that God sees your heart, thoughts and desires? Why? How do you strive to align yourself with God's will for you?

4 Why do you think we sometimes change our behaviour when we know that others are watching us? When have you been surprised that someone was observing your actions?

5 Name the scripture passages, spiritual practices and people that most encourage you to align your heart with your actions. How do they help? How does it feel when your heart and actions are aligned?

Wednesday 3 November

1 How often do you berate yourself for something you have said or done? Do you find it easy to let go of mistakes? What mistake has been most challenging for you to move beyond?

2 Describe a time when God spoke to your heart and changed your mindset. What changes occurred? What did you learn about God from this experience?

3 Why do you think negative thoughts can easily exhaust us? In what ways can praising God energise us? When have you noticed praise changing your attitude and energy level the most?

4 What helps you to keep your heart and thoughts focused on God? Name the scripture passages, spiritual practices and activities that best help you stay focused on the Almighty.

5 How does having a God-focused mindset allow you to live faithfully and serve others?

Wednesday 10 November

1 Have you ever been about to discard something, only to have someone tell you it is exactly what they need? What do experiences like these teach us about the value of what is around us? What do they teach us about ourselves?

2 Where do you look for reminders of your value when you are feeling overlooked or unimportant? How does your faith community remind you of your value to God?

3 Name something about yourself that you tend to devalue, but that has great value to God and to those around you. Why do you devalue it? How does God remind you of its value?

4 Who in the Bible seemed unimportant outwardly, yet God said otherwise? How does this person's story remind you of God's ability to use what we reject in order to change the world? How does this story encourage you in your daily life?

5 In what ways do you actively look for the blessings others have to offer? How do you help them see the value and make the most of those blessings?

Wednesday 17 November

1 When does the noise of the world frustrate or distract you? When is it hardest for you to hear God amid the distractions?

2 Where do you find peace from distractions? How often do you set aside quiet time for yourself? In what ways does quiet feel comfortable, and in what ways does quiet challenge you?

3 Do you make space for spiritual reflection in your daily routine? If so, how do daily pauses strengthen your relationship with God? If not, would you consider making this a practice?

4 Name a biblical character who listened for and heard God's voice. What can we learn from them about the importance of listening for God? How does their experience hearing God's voice differ from your experience? How is it similar?

5 How are you intentional about listening for God speaking to you? How do you know when God is speaking to you? How do you avoid missing God's voice?

Wednesday 24 November

1 Do you find it less overwhelming to accomplish a large task when you break it into smaller steps? Why or why not? Have you ever applied the same strategy to your faith journey?

2 Describe a time when you observed small parts making a difference to the whole. What can this teach us about the importance of each moment and choice we make?

3 What does the phrase 'Give your life to Jesus' mean to you? Do you find it helpful or do you prefer more specific examples of how you might better follow Christ?

4 How do you take advantage of the small opportunities to obey God each day? In what ways are the small chances to obey as important as the big ones?

5 Who in your life encourages you to follow God in big ways and small ways? How do they encourage you? How can you encourage others in a similar way?

Wednesday 1 December

1 Recall a time when you felt anxious or unable to sleep before an event. What did you do? How did you find peace?

2 Which scripture passages encourage you the most when you are worried or anxious?

3 In what ways do you reach out to God in times of anxiety? How do your prayers, devotional times and spiritual disciplines in times of uncertainty differ from these practices in times of peace?

4 Think of someone in your life who is going through a time of uncertainty. How can you encourage them? Name some ways you can show them friendship and God's love and care.

5 When have you come across a Bible passage that gave you exactly what you needed during a difficult time? What did this teach you about God's presence and provision?

Wednesday 8 December

1 Why do you think we sometimes feel afraid in the dark but safe in the light? Where do you turn for comfort and safety when you are afraid?

2 Imagine the world without literal light. Now imagine the world without spiritual light. Which one is more frightening to you? What do these images teach you about the importance of light in the world?

3 How does the story of Jesus' birth encourage you during frightening times? What other stories of God's power and light encourage you when you are afraid?

4 What prayers and spiritual practices help you to remember and appreciate God's light throughout the Christmas season? What scripture passages are your favorites this time of year?

5 Name some specific ways that you can spread God's light of love this week. In what ways will you be intentional about shining brightly in the lives of others?

Wednesday 15 December

1 When have you been upset about a situation, only to have your perspective changed by someone? How did your new attitude change how you felt about your situation?

2 When you feel stressed, do you find it difficult to remain focused on God? What brings your focus back to God?

3 Name some scripture passages that speak about the importance of remaining open to serving God in all circumstances. Which of these passages is most encouraging for you?

4 When have you found an unexpected opportunity to serve God and others? What was your experience? How was your faith enriched by your service?

5 How do your spiritual mentors help you to find ways to serve God? How does your church community encourage you to serve?

Wednesday 22 December

1 What helps you to remain positive and joyful about what God is doing in your life when you do not receive the outcome that you had hoped for? What scripture passages give you the most encouragement about God's plan for your life?

2 When have you waited for a miracle that did not come? How did this affect your trust and faith in God? What encouraging words would you offer someone waiting for a miracle?

3 What miracle of acceptance and faith can you thank God for today? What would help you to take more notice of God's miracles each day?

4 How are you encouraged to know that God will never leave you? How does this knowledge strengthen your faith?

5 As you and your faith community pray for miracles, how can you also encourage acceptance and faith regardless of the outcomes? How will you remind one another of the unexpected and daily miracles you encounter?

Wednesday 29 December

1 Recall a time when you felt the presence of God in a new and different way. How did that experience change your relationship with God? How did the experience change you?

2 Have you ever wished that God would simply fix your problems rather than change you? Why? What helps you to accept and appreciate the ways God changes you, even if God does not miraculously change your circumstances?

3 When is it easiest for you to follow Christ's teachings? When is it hardest? Where do you find strength to follow Christ even when it is difficult?

4 What does it mean to you to be transformed by God? How does transformation allow us to better serve God and others? For what transformations in your life are you most grateful?

5 What changes do you think we would see in the world if we all became more Christlike? How can you participate in making this a reality? Name some specific steps you will take to become more Christlike today.

Journal page

Introducing BRF's advocates lead

Jane Butcher has been BRF's advocates lead since September 2020. Jane is no stranger to BRF, having joined the team 13 years ago working with Barnabas in Schools and our Children and Families ministry.

As BRF seeks to further develop and celebrate volunteering across the organisation, one of Jane's key roles is to work with our volunteer managers to ensure all our volunteers have a rewarding and enjoyable experience with BRF. She also hopes to encourage more people to join us by raising awareness of our volunteer opportunities.

Jane is also gathering a team of volunteer advocates to share the work of BRF – our ministries, resources and support offering – in their local church and surrounding area.

Could you help or do you know someone who could?

Whether you have a little or a lot of time, previous experience of advocating or none, we would love to hear from you! We are looking for people of all ages who have a heart for what BRF does to help us raise awareness of our work and invite even more people to be a part of it.

All BRF volunteers can be assured of a warm welcome, ongoing support and appreciation as a valued part of our team.

If you or anyone you know might be interested in becoming an advocate for BRF, please email Jane at **jane.butcher@brf.org.uk**.

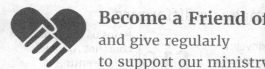

Become a Friend of BRF

and give regularly
to support our ministry

We help people of all ages to grow in faith

We encourage and support individual Christians and churches as they serve and resource the changing spiritual needs of communities today.

Through **Anna Chaplaincy**
we're enabling churches to provide
spiritual care to older people

Through **Living Faith**
we're nurturing faith and resourcing
life-long discipleship

Through **Messy Church**
we're helping churches to reach out
to families

Through **Parenting for Faith**
we're supporting parents as they raise
their children in the Christian faith

Our ministry is only possible because of the generous support of individuals, churches, trusts and gifts in wills.

As we look to the future and make plans, **regular donations make a huge difference** in ensuring we can both start and finish projects well.

By becoming a Friend of BRF and giving regularly to our ministry you are partnering with us in the gospel and helping change lives.

How your gift makes a difference

£2 a month	Helps us to develop **Living Faith** resources to use in care homes and communities	**£10** a month	Helps us to support churches running the **Parenting for Faith** course and stand alongside parents
£5 a month	Helps us to support **Messy Church** volunteers and resource and grow the wider network	**£20** a month	Helps us to resource **Anna Chaplaincy** and improve spiritual care for older people

 # How to become a Friend of BRF

Set up a Direct Debit donation at **brf.org.uk/donate** or find out how to set up a Standing Order at **brf.org.uk/friends**

Contact the fundraising team

Email: **giving@brf.org.uk**
Tel: +44 (0)1235 462305
Post: Fundraising team, BRF, 15 The Chambers, Vineyard, Abingdon OX14 3FE

Good to know

If you have any questions, or if you want to change your regular donation or stop giving in the future, do get in touch.

Registered with

FR

FUNDRAISING **REGULATOR**

SHARING OUR VISION – MAKING A ONE-OFF GIFT

I would like to make a donation to support BRF.
Please use my gift for:

☐ Where it is most needed ☐ Anna Chaplaincy ☐ Living Faith

☐ Messy Church ☐ Parenting for Faith

Title	First name/initials	Surname	
Address			
			Postcode
Email			
Telephone			
Signature			Date

Our ministry is only possible because of the generous support of individuals, churches, trusts and gifts in wills.

giftaid it You can add an extra 25p to every £1 you give.

Please treat as Gift Aid donations all qualifying gifts of money made

☐ today, ☐ in the past four years, ☐ and in the future.

I am a UK taxpayer and understand that if I pay less Income Tax and/or Capital Gains Tax in the current tax year than the amount of Gift Aid claimed on all my donations, it is my responsibility to pay any difference.

☐ My donation does not qualify for Gift Aid.

Please notify BRF if you want to cancel this Gift Aid declaration, change your name or home address, or no longer pay sufficient tax on your income and/or capital gains.

Please complete other side of form ➲

SHARING OUR VISION – MAKING A ONE-OFF GIFT

Please accept my gift of:

☐ £2 ☐ £5 ☐ £10 ☐ £20 Other £ [   ]

by (*delete as appropriate*):

☐ Cheque/Charity Voucher payable to 'BRF'

☐ MasterCard/Visa/Debit card/Charity card

Name on card

Card no. [   ] [   ] [   ] [   ]

Expires end [MM] [YY] Security code* [   ]

*Last 3 digits on the reverse of the card
ESSENTIAL IN ORDER TO PROCESS
YOUR PAYMENT

Signature | Date

☐ I would like to leave a gift to BRF in my will.
Please send me further information.

For help or advice regarding making a gift, please contact
our fundraising team +44 (0)1865 462305

Your privacy

We will use your personal data to process this transaction.
From time to time we may send you information about the
work of BRF that we think may be of interest to you. Our
privacy policy is available at **brf.org.uk/privacy**. Please
contact us if you wish to discuss your mailing preferences.

Registered with

FUNDRAISING
REGULATOR

↻ Please complete other side of form

Please return this form to 'Freepost BRF'
No other address information or stamp is needed

The Bible Reading Fellowship is a Registered Charity (233280)

UR0321

Grab a cuppa and sink into a cosy chair as a father–daughter duo leads you into the celebration of Christmas through their art and reflections. Considering not only the story of Mary and Joseph journeying to Bethlehem, where Jesus was born, but also our modern-day expressions of Christmas, they bring light and life to what can be a fraught and exhausting season. A book perfect for giving as a gift or using oneself to foster joy and peace.

Celebrating Christmas
Embracing joy through art and reflections
Amy Boucher Pye, illustrations by Leo Boucher
978 1 80039 051 5 £8.99
brfonline.org.uk

The Bible is at the heart of BRF's work, and this special anniversary collection is a celebration of the Bible for BRF's centenary year. Bringing together a fantastically wide-ranging writing team of authors, supporters and well-wishers from all areas of BRF's work, this resource is designed to help us go deeper into the story of the Bible and reflect on how we can share it in our everyday lives. Including sections which lead us through the Bible narrative as well as thematic and seasonal sections, it is the perfect daily companion to resource your spiritual journey.

The BRF Book of 365 Bible Reflections
with contributions from BRF authors, supporters and well-wishers
978 1 80039 100 0 £14.99
brfonline.org.uk

How to encourage Bible reading in your church

BRF has been helping individuals connect with the Bible for nearly a century. We want to support churches as they seek to encourage church members into regular Bible reading.

Order a Bible reading resources pack

This pack is designed to give your church the tools to publicise our Bible reading notes. It includes:

- Sample Bible reading notes for your congregation to try.
- Publicity resources, including a poster.
- A church magazine feature about Bible reading notes.

The pack is free, but we welcome a £5 donation to cover the cost of postage. If you require a pack to be sent outside the UK or require a specific number of sample Bible reading notes, please contact us for postage costs. More information about what the current pack contains is available on our website.

How to order and find out more

- Visit **brfonline.org.uk/resourcespack**.
- Telephone BRF on +44 (0)1865 319700 Mon–Fri 9.30–17.00.
- Write to us at BRF, 15 The Chambers, Vineyard, Abingdon OX14 3FE.

Keep informed about our latest initiatives

We are continuing to develop resources to help churches encourage people into regular Bible reading, wherever they are on their journey. Join our email list at **brfonline.org.uk/signup** to stay informed about the latest initiatives that your church could benefit from.

Subscriptions

The Upper Room is published in January, May and September.

Individual subscriptions
The subscription rate for orders for 4 or fewer copies includes postage and packing:

The Upper Room annual individual subscription   £18.00

Group subscriptions
Orders for 5 copies or more, sent to ONE address, are post free:
The Upper Room annual group subscription   £14.25

Please do not send payment with order for a group subscription. We will send an invoice with your first order.

Please note that the annual billing period for group subscriptions runs from 1 May to 30 April.

Copies of the notes may also be obtained from Christian bookshops.

Single copies of *The Upper Room* cost £4.75.

Prices valid until 30 April 2022.

Giant print version
The Upper Room is available in giant print for the visually impaired, from:

Torch Trust for the Blind
Torch House
Torch Way
Northampton Road
Market Harborough   Tel: +44 (0)1858 438260
LE16 9HL   **torchtrust.org**

THE UPPER ROOM: INDIVIDUAL/GIFT SUBSCRIPTION FORM

All our Bible reading notes can be ordered online by visiting brfonline.org.uk/subscriptions

☐ I would like to take out a subscription myself (complete your name and address details once)

☐ I would like to give a gift subscription (please provide both names and addresses)

Title .... First name/initials .... Surname ....

Address ....

.... Postcode ....

Telephone .... Email ....

Gift subscription name ....

Gift subscription address ....

.... Postcode ....

Gift message (20 words max. or include your own gift card):

....

....

Please send *The Upper Room* beginning with the January 2022 / May 2022 / September 2022 issue (*delete as appropriate*):

Annual individual subscription ☐ £18.00

Optional donation* to support the work of BRF £ ....

Total enclosed £ .... (cheques should be made payable to 'BRF')

*Please complete and return the Gift Aid declaration on page 159 to make your donation even more valuable to us.

Method of payment

☐ Cheque (made payable to BRF) ☐ MasterCard / Visa

Card no. ☐☐☐☐ ☐☐☐☐ ☐☐☐☐ ☐☐☐☐

Expires end ☐☐ ☐☐ M M Y Y   Security code* ☐☐☐   Last 3 digits on the reverse of the card

*ESSENTIAL IN ORDER TO PROCESS THE PAYMENT

UR0321

> **All our Bible reading notes can be ordered online by visiting brfonline.org.uk/subscriptions**

❑ Please send me .... copies of *The Upper Room* January 2022 / May 2022 / September 2022 issue (*delete as appropriate*)

Title .... First name/initials .... Surname ....

Address ....

.... Postcode ....

Telephone .... Email ....

Please do not send payment with this order. We will send an invoice with your first order.

Christian bookshops: All good Christian bookshops stock BRF publications. For your nearest stockist, please contact BRF.

Telephone: The BRF office is open Mon–Fri 9.30–17.00. To place your order, telephone +44 (0)1865 319700.

Online: brfonline.org.uk/group-subscriptions

❑ Please send me a Bible reading resources pack to encourage Bible reading in my church

Please return this form with the appropriate payment to:
BRF, 15 The Chambers, Vineyard, Abingdon OX14 3FE
To read our terms and find out about cancelling your order, please visit **brfonline.org.uk/terms**.

The Bible Reading Fellowship is a Registered Charity (233280)

To order

Online: **brfonline.org.uk**
Telephone: +44 (0)1865 319700 Mon–Fri 9.30–17.00

Delivery times within the UK are normally 15 working days. Prices are correct at the time of going to press but may change without prior notice.

Title	Price	Qty	Total
Celebrating Christmas	£8.99		
The BRF Book of 365 Bible Reflections	£14.99		

POSTAGE AND PACKING CHARGES			
Order value	UK	Europe	Rest of world
Under £7.00	£2.00	Available on request	Available on request
£7.00–£29.99	£3.00		
£30.00 and over	FREE		

Total value of books	
Postage and packing	
Donation*	
Total for this order	

* Please complete the Gift Aid declaration below

Please complete in BLOCK CAPITALS

Title .... First name/initials .... Surname...

Address ....

.... Postcode ....

Acc. No. .... Telephone ....

Email ....

The Bible Reading Fellowship Gift Aid Declaration

giftaid it

Please treat as Gift Aid donations all qualifying gifts of money made

❑ today, ❑ in the past four years, ❑ and in the future **or** ❑ My donation does not qualify for Gift Aid.

I am a UK taxpayer and understand that if I pay less Income Tax and/or Capital Gains Tax in the current tax year than the amount of Gift Aid claimed on all my donations, it is my responsibility to pay any difference.

Please notify BRF if you want to cancel this declaration, change your name or home address, or no longer pay sufficient tax on your income and/or capital gains.

Method of payment

❑ Cheque (made payable to BRF) ❑ MasterCard / Visa

Card no. ☐☐☐☐ ☐☐☐☐ ☐☐☐☐ ☐☐☐☐ ☐☐☐☐

Expires end ☐☐ M M ☐☐ Y Y Security code* ☐☐☐ Last 3 digits on the reverse of the card

Signature* .... Date .... /.......... /..........

*ESSENTIAL IN ORDER TO PROCESS THE PAYMENT

Please return this form to: BRF, 15 The Chambers, Vineyard, Abingdon OX14 3FE | **enquiries@brf.org.uk**

To read our terms and find out about cancelling your order, please visit **brfonline.org.uk/terms**.

The Bible Reading Fellowship (BRF) is a Registered Charity (233280)

Enabling all ages to grow in faith

Anna Chaplaincy
Living Faith
Messy Church
Parenting for Faith

The Bible Reading Fellowship (BRF) is a Christian charity that resources individuals and churches. Our vision is to enable people of all ages to grow in faith and understanding of the Bible and to see more people equipped to exercise their gifts in leadership and ministry.

To find out more about our work, visit
brf.org.uk